THE
OVERCOMERS

These are . . .
THE OVERCOMERS

TOM LANDRY Head Coach, Dallas Cowboys

TERRY BRADSHAW Quarterback, Pittsburgh Steelers

CRAIG MORTON Quarterback, Denver Broncos

KYLE ROTE, JR. Superstars Champion (soccer)

MADELINE JACKSON Olympic Champion (800-meter)

JOHN HAVLICEK Basketball All-Pro, Boston Celtics

MEL KENYON Race Car Champion

EARL CAMPBELL Heisman Trophy Winner

CINDY POTTER McINGVALE Olympic Diver

DANNY THOMPSON late infielder, Texas Rangers

JANET LYNN Figure Skating Champion

JIM RYUN Champion Miler

HARRY CORDELLOS Blind Marathon Runner

Profiles of Christian Athletes
Who Became...

THE OVERCOMERS

Carlton Stowers

WORD BOOKS
PUBLISHER
WACO, TEXAS

THE OVERCOMERS

ISBN 0–8499–2837–0

Library of Congress catalog card number: 78-58594

Printed in the United States of America

For
THE REV. DEAN PRATT . . .
an overcomer in his own right

Acknowledgments:

Some of the material in this book previously appeared in slightly different form. The chapters on the late Danny Thompson and Earl Campbell first appeared in *Scene,* the Sunday magazine of the *Dallas Morning News*. The chapter on Cindy Potter McIngvale was originally published in *womenSports* magazine. That these publications have allowed the stories to be included in this collection is greatly appreciated.

Photo credits: Morton, Denver Broncos photo; Rote, John Rhodes photo; Havlicek, Boston Celtics photo; Campbell, *Dallas News;* McIngvale, Wide World Photo; Thompson, Larry Reese photo; Lynn, Wide World Photo; Ryun, Wide World Photo; Cordellos, Larry Reese photo.

CONTENTS

Acknowledgments
Introduction   9
TOM LANDRY—Head Coach, Dallas Cowboys   15
CRAIG MORTON—Quarterback, Denver Broncos   25
TERRY BRADSHAW—Quarterback, Pittsburgh
    Steelers   38
KYLE ROTE, JR.—Superstars Champion (Soccer)   50
MADELINE MANNING JACKSON—Olympic Champion
    (800-meter run)   61
JOHN HAVLICEK—All-Pro, Boston Celtics   72
MEL KENYON—Three-time Midget Race Car
    Champion   83
EARL CAMPBELL—1977 Heisman Trophy Winner   91
CINDY POTTER MCINGVALE—Olympic Diver   103
DANNY THOMPSON—Infielder, Texas Rangers   110
JANET LYNN—Five-time U. S. Women's Champion
    (Figure skating)   122
JIM RYUN—Miler   131
HARRY CORDELLOS—Blind Marathon Runner   144

INTRODUCTION

SPORT, whether on sandlots or in stadiums seating thousands, is, it has been said, the act of heroism constantly repeating itself. Basically, that is what draws us, young and old, to the ball parks, the sports pages, and the weekend telecasts. We are and likely forever will be a nation in search of new heroes. As each new sports season begins, new ones come to our attention, constantly crowding the old, established heroes for the attention of the American sports followers.

This, then, is a book about heroes. It is a book about men and women who, through dedication, courage, long hours of hard work and abiding faith have used their God-given talents to achieve the kinds of victories which prompt appreciation and more than a little awe from those of us who look on from sideline vantage points. It is a book about Olympic champions and Heisman Trophy winners, world record holders, Super Bowl victors and athletes who have overcome crushing setbacks to find their spot on the winner's stand. It is a book which devotes considerable attention to the courageous nature of a group of unique people who happen also to be gifted athletes. If there is a central theme which binds the chapters together it is one of humility maintained in the almost constant glare of the public spotlight. In another day we called it simple modesty, a characteristic which at times seems to be sadly absent in the modern day sports arena. None of the athletes profiled on these pages have ever served as their own public relations men nor have they predicted victory for themselves even before the competition was begun. Neither will you find anyone here who has advanced his or her own cause by taking unfair advantage of another. Yet they have collectively triumphed in their respective fields of sport.

There are, in fact, victories described which never earned the winner a picture on the cover of *Sports Illustrated* or caused the Lions Club back in his home town to throw a banquet.

As one tries to view the overall picture of sport he must wonder how much greater, really, the achievement of a Terry Bradshaw leading the Pittsburgh Steelers to the Super Bowl title is than that of Harry Cordellos, the blind information clerk, as he completed the demanding twenty-six-mile Boston Marathon in less than three hours. For his accomplishment, Bradshaw received a check for over $17,000. Cordellos earned a bowl of hot beef stew and a medal. Yet, in a sense, they stand on equal ground. Both are champions, men of rare accomplishment. Each had followed the credo of the late John F. Kennedy who said, "I have to go flat out, to do my best." Each had done so—and along the way had the insight to realize that he had not achieved his triumph by himself.

Danny Thompson, major league infielder, could not have fought his youthful battle with a fatal disease by himself, continuing to play ball despite the fact his days were numbered. Mel Kenyon needed something more than his own competitive will to return to auto racing after being seriously burned in an accident.

Each had God in his life.

As a follower of sports all of my professional life and witness to many of the events which have sent the American public into a hand-wringing frenzy, it has been my good fortune to have come in contact with a number of athletes from all walks of sporting life. Those about whom I've chosen to write in this book are special. As you read about them, I think you'll see why.

—CARLTON STOWERS

THE
OVERCOMERS

TOM LANDRY

Head Coach, Dallas Cowboys

TO THE SOUTH an unseasonal, gloomy fog was roll-
ing in, blocking out the late afternoon Dallas skyline.
Most downtown office buildings had already emptied, al-
lowing workers to escape to the maze of freeways and
turnpikes which somehow, amazingly, manage to lead

them home. In the bumper-to-bumper traffic many drivers were no doubt listening to the radio stations' taped version of an announcement Dallas Cowboys head coach Tom Landry had made at a noon press conference.

". . . and so," he had said, "I have selected Roger Staubach as our No. 1 quarterback . . . ."

He knew there would be those who were pleased with the choice; there would be those who weren't; and then there would be those—the majority probably—who were happy for the pure and simple reason that *some* decision had at last been made.

It had been mid-season and the Cowboys, piloted first by Craig Morton, then Staubach, then Morton-Staubach and Staubach-Morton, were again floundering aimlessly —a team with a wealth of talent but no sense of direction.

Now it was later in the day, in the relative quiet of the Cowboys' practice field. The workout had been light, snappy, and generally pleasing. Players were hurriedly showering and dressing as Landry remained outside, jogging his customary post-practice laps, then stopping to reflect for the benefit of a lone questioning writer, on the decision he had announced earlier in the day.

He spoke candidly, in quiet, almost whisper-like tones. "Sometimes," he said, "this job isn't much fun. I just pray that I've done the right thing."

For Thomas Wade Landry, the man who has been at the Cowboys' helm from the dog days of 1960 to the Super Bowl '70s, it was an uncharacteristic admission. For that brief moment in the damp twilight of a deserted practice field the certainty, the ironclad self-assurance of the confident computerman slipped over into the gray area where you and I live day after day. He had done what he thought was best but without the benefit of any guarantees, any green light from tendency charts or computer tapes. Tom Landry, at long last, had taken a gamble—and in doing so, he approached mortality.

Thus, one must add still another side to the many dimensional man, the enigma of sports world enigmas. To accept an assignment to write about Tom Landry is to expose one's self to a myriad of complexities. It is not greatly unlike retreating to the almost forgotten boyhood days of ghost-chasing and snipe hunts.

As the Cowboys have evolved steadily into one of professional football's perennial giants, the stature of the Landry mystique has also grown.

There was a time, fifteen years ago, when the team was composed mostly of disillusioned veterans with their heydays in the past. Then he was referred to as Pope Landry I, the man with the deep religious convictions who neither smoked, sipped spirits, nor spoke profanely. He had, it was often said, the personality of a tombstone and his idea of a high old time was an eighteen-hour workday and a Max Brand western on plane trips home from games.

"Tom," Cowboys president Tex Schramm once said, "isn't the easiest man in the world to communicate with. You sometimes have to hit him with a two-by-four to get his attention, but once you've got it, you get his whole attention. He has rare perspective. For instance, he is known as a progressive coach, yet in a lot of ways he's very conservative."

There are those who will have you add the adjective humorless. And impersonal. And emotionless. And, finally, in the words of an outspoken sage, Duane Thomas, "a plastic man; no man at all." It goes on and on.

You look at him, this balding, high-cheeked, fiftyish

man of dapper dress, firm convictions, and meticulous manner, and feel compelled to ask the real Tom Landry to please stand up, to show some sign of who he is, what he is really all about. The best you can hope for is the engaging flick of a smile, that of a mischievous little boy. Still another Tom (Tommy, maybe?) Landry.

Perhaps no coach in professional sports has been praised and verbally bombarded with such seasonal regularity as Landry. Undoubtedly longevity is part of the reason. Since the city gained an NFL franchise in 1960, Landry has been the coach—the only coach—of the Dallas Cowboys. He is as much a fixture in Big D as Neiman-Marcus or the State Fairgrounds. With him at the controls, the Cowboys have taken a roller-coaster ride to the top, stumbling one Sunday, looking very much like a dynasty the next. Since 1965 no team has produced a better won-lost record than Landry's Cowboys. And no team has a coach who has been the subject of so much second-guessing.

His philosophy on the subject is grass roots simple. "Actually, it's something of a status symbol," he explains. "We have reached a point where our fans feel we are capable of and should in fact win every game we play. They are frustrated with anything less. So they have to have someone to take that frustration out on. That's me."

Were one to take a poll among the anti-Landry element in Dallas and the pro football world, there would be two distinct complaints—one professional, the other more personal.

Grandstand quarterbacks, educated by Howard Cosell, newspaper columnists, and a couple of sports paperbacks they picked up at the drug store, question the complexities of the multiple offense and the famed 4–3 flex defense, both products of Landry's innovative imagination. Time was when there were those, rival coaches included, who questioned the Cowboys' near scientific approach. Today, many of them have jumped on the bandwagon and are borrowing freely from the Dallas playbook.

"Tom," says New Orleans Saints coach Dick Nolan, "hasn't received all the credit he should have. He's far and away the smartest man in the game today. He's forgotten more than most of us will ever be able to learn."

"Nobody," adds former New York Giants coach Alex Webster, "is smarter than Tom Landry."

So, if you're keeping score, make it Landry, The Coach, 1; Grandstand Quarterbacks, 0.

The most constant and repetitive attacks have been leveled at Landry, the cold, emotionless man whose impassive expressions have puzzled TV viewers for years.

A former Cowboys defensive back once made this observation: "He would never pat you on the behind and tell you you had done a good job. If you intercepted a pass or recovered a fumble, he looked at you as if to say, that's what you're supposed to do. By the same token, he never really chewed you out when you messed up. You just never knew where you stood with the man."

All-Pro linebacker Chuck Howley, now retired, recalls the first time he had occasion to visit Landry in his office: "I went in," he says, "and Tom was looking out the window, and I bet I was there five minutes before he ever knew it. But now he seems to be a little looser. He's more friendly. He even speaks to you when he passes you now."

Which is not to say life among the Cowboys has become one big fraternity party, but there is good reason to believe Landry has made some attempt to escape the stone man image which has been attached to him.

Even he admits that there has been some change:

"I do feel more at ease with myself," he says. "Maybe it's because I'm getting older.

"I think the impression of coldness people have had of me comes mostly during a game. A good coach can be a cheerleader, I suppose. But if he's really involved and concentrating the way he has to to make the necessary decisions and corrections I just don't see how he can be running around yelling and slapping people on the back. Distractions can ruin decisions you have to make on the sidelines.

"I'm very meticulous. Everything has to fit perfectly in our scheme of things. If something is out of kilter I don't like it and I want it corrected as soon as possible."

Which is why he runs his sidelines like Inspection Day at Ft. Dix. From kickoff to final gun he is pulling the strings, running the show. It is his manner to stand above and beyond the rest. The aloofness which comes through to your living room is no accident.

Except for the practice field, meeting room or sideline, Landry permits himself little personal contact with players. It is more a device of self-protection than one of coldness. Decisions, like the one which sent Craig Morton to the bench in favor of Staubach, are easier made if one does not let personal involvement play a role.

"I've read where he says he doesn't feel it is good to get too close to the players," says wide receiver Drew Pearson, "and I suppose that is the way it has to be. But I'll tell you this: He cares. He cares a lot. He believes in treating people like people and no man who feels that way can be as cold as some people believe him to be."

Score: Landry, The Man, 2; Grandstand Quarterbacks, zip.

Football, to be sure, is not the Alpha and Omega of the Tom Landry story. Ahead of his devotion to winning comes his religion, the old-fashioned, man-and-his-God relationship which might, to some, seem out of place in professional football's jet-set violence. To Landry, God is very real, a driving force in his life.

"I grew up in a Christian home," he says, "but I wasn't truly converted to Christ until 1958. I had tried to live a moral life but I wasn't a true Christian. Most people go through life always looking, seeking. I found out that a Christian commitment is the only real purpose in life."

A member of the Highland Park United Methodist Church, he helped organize a man's Bible study group several years ago and regularly attends the 7:30 A.M. Thursday sessions. He has served as the national president of the Fellowship of Christian Athletes and was the general chairman of a recent Greater Southwest Billy Graham Crusade.

"I find great enjoyment in working in things like the FCA," he is quick to point out. "It's my obligation as a Christian to do what I can to spread the word. In speeches I make I just try to tell how religion works in my life and enters into whatever I do. I say the basic things it takes to be a champion in sports are the basic things it takes to be a champion for God.

"Without my faith," he continues, "I'd be in real bad shape. Faith gives a man hope and this, to me, is the thing life is all about.

"I begin each day with a person-to-Person contact with Him. 'Lord, I need your help today when we make squad cuts,' or 'Please give me the right words to say to the coaches at our meeting,' or, 'Help me forget football today when I'm with my family.' "

He is not, however, one to flaunt his convictions. "If," says an assistant coach, "Tom has ever saved any souls he did it quietly, without anyone else knowing. That's his way."

Then, there is his family: wife, Alicia, whom he met and married while attending the University of Texas, son Tom, Jr., and daughters, Kitty and Lisa.

"Tom," says Mrs. Landry, "is a good father. He somehow manages to work everything in and still leave some time for his family." In the off-season he makes an attempt to keep his weekends as free as possible from coaching and speaking duties and arranges his days off so that they will fall on family occasions such as anniversaries and birthdays.

Football, however, has been a major part of his life since he was a youngster growing up in Mission, Texas, the son of the chief of the Volunteer Fire Department.

"Mission was a great place to grow up," he says, "I learned some valuable things playing in the sandlots— things that many of today's youngsters aren't fortunate enough to experience. Here is where a boy learns to cry and fight and overcome all kinds of situations according to his own abilities and initiatives."

In his senior year at Mission High he was an all-regional fullback and safetyman on a team which went 12–0 and wasn't scored on.

He was a standout member of the University of Texas team, taking time out to fly a B-17 during the war. His college days complete and Alicia Wiggs Landry in tow, he went to New York where he played six seasons as a cornerback for the New York Giants (1950–55), the last four as a player-coach.

Following his retirement as an active player he remained with the Giants as a full-time defensive coach until 1959.

Thus, the man who by training was to have been an industrial engineer, had committed himself to a life's work.

Wellington Mara, owner of the Giants, once compared the coaching techniques of Landry and another assistant who was working on the Giants staff—Vince Lombardi.

"Lombardi," he says, "was a much warmer person. He went from warm to red hot. You could hear him laughing or shouting for five blocks. You couldn't hear Tom from the next chair. Lombardi, in some ways, was more of a teacher. It was as though Tom lectured to the upper 40 percent of the class and Lombardi lectured to the lower 10 percent."

Landry, then, has come up through the ranks—player, player-coach, assistant coach, head coach—bringing with him an intellectual approach to his chosen craft.

"The day Landry quit playing and became a full-time coach," says former teammate Frank Gifford, "it was as if he had been coaching twenty years. I doubt that there has ever been anyone who was more a student of the game."

What has evolved is a man who is regarded as one of the very best in his field. His methods may differ from others, his style sometimes may seem too orthodox, then totally unorthodox, yet he is a winner among winners.

"Nothing checks his confidence," says Cowboys assistant Jim Myers, "neither early failure, success or anything. He has more humility in defeat or victory than anyone I ever saw."

If one were to take on the impossible task of pinpointing the day Landry did in fact begin to relax he could do no worse than retreat to the ice palace of Green Bay, Wisconsin, when the Lombardi Packers defeated the Cowboys in the waning seconds of the 1967 NFL championship game.

A week later Landry stood before a gathering in San Antonio and without so much as a trace of a grin, said, "You can tell the real Cowboys—they're the ones with the frozen hands and the broken hearts." It brought the house down.

His dry wit was still in evidence the following summer when the Cowboys gathered in Thousand Oaks, California, for training camp. Don Meredith was working on his passing, throwing at a target from a distance of fifteen yards and having trouble hitting the mark. In frustration he watched as one hit well to the left, then said, "Well, I'll be a S.O.B. . . ."

Landry, happening by, did not slow his pace or even look in Dandy Don's direction. He simply remarked, "That, I'm afraid, would not help your passing one bit. . . ."

No cold, emotionless, humorless, plastic man could have come up with a one-liner like that.

Score another one for Landry.

CRAIG MORTON

Quarterback, Denver Broncos

THE LAST REMNANTS of summer still hung in the air as the Dallas Cowboys wound up their 1971 exhibition schedule with a 24–17 victory over the Kansas City Chiefs which was not assured until the final minutes of play. A crowd of 74,000 had echoed its approval through the Cotton Bowl as Craig Morton, the team's new quarterback since the retirement of Don Meredith, threw a last-minute touchdown pass to clinch the victory.

In the postgame dressing room Morton was surrounded by sportswriters eager to gain his observations on the game's dramatic conclusion. The youthful quarterback patiently answered the questions and, once satisfied that the attending journalists had what they needed for the next morning's editions, said, "Gentlemen, if you will excuse me now, I've got to run. I have an important date." Having thus ended the interview, he smiled and pulled on a windbreaker.

The writers returned the smile and exchanged knowing glances. Morton, they knew, ranked as one of Dallas' most eligible bachelors, a familiar face among the city's "in crowd." A man in love with the good life, he favored beautiful women, expensive clothes, spur-of-the-moment ski trips to Aspen, and riding the back roads astride his high-powered motorcycle. Given time, many assumed, Craig Morton could be to Dallas what Joe Namath was to New York. An athlete all had at one time or another described as a swinger, Craig Morton was no doubt off to celebrate his game-winning performance in high style.

The truth of the matter was that he had to catch a plane for San Antonio.

He had received a call earlier from a San Antonio sportswriter named Dan Cook, telling him of the plight of an eleven-year-old Dallas Cowboys fan named Bill Miller, a youngster bedridden—and dying—with leukemia.

Bill's dad, urgently seeking ways to make his son's life as complete as possible, had asked the youngster what he would like most to do. "I would," the weakened boy replied, "like to meet Craig Morton." The elder Miller immediately sought out the local sports editor for advice. "Let me call Craig," Cook had suggested.

Morton heard the request and immediately said he would do whatever he could. "I only have two favors to ask," Craig said. First, he asked that Cook and the youngster's dad meet him at the airport so they could talk about Bill on the way to the Santa Rosa Hospital. "And," the former University of California All-American added, "let's keep this just between us. No publicity."

"Fair enough," Cook replied.

Thus that evening Morton, wearing a surgical mask and gown and walking softly, entered the sterile room where young Bill lay sleeping. He went over to the bed and touched the boy's shoulder. "Hi, Bill," he said, "I'm Craig Morton."

The weakened youngster stared for a few moments, not saying a word, then finally spoke. "Aw, you're kidding me," he said. "You aren't really Craig Morton, are you?"

Morton pulled down the surgical mask to reveal the face young Bill Miller had seen only in newspaper photos and on the television screen. Morton winked.

The 6'-4", 210-pound quarterback then sat on the edge of the bed and spoke quietly to his young fan as an appreciative mother and father looked on. He had brought along a football autographed by all the members of the Cowboys' team. The two talked and laughed, not as strangers, but as friends. Finally, Morton turned to the others in the room. "I would," he said softly, "appreciate it if everyone would leave us alone for a few minutes."

The parents and the nurse obediently turned for the door. Morton gave them a reassuring smile as they left.

Several minutes passed before he came out into the

hall where the evicted guests waited. "Who is nurse Margaret?" Morton asked. A shy black nurse stepped forward.

"Margaret," Craig said, "we've got a real problem that needs to be straightened out right away."

"What seems to be the matter?" she asked.

"From now on," Morton grinned, "Bill has got to have more gravy on his potatoes. Okay?"

"Okay."

With that Morton returned to the boy's side for another few minutes of visiting. He then told his new-found friend good-by and left for the airport and his return trip to Dallas. He never revealed the nature of the conversation to anyone but later Bill would tell his father that "they talked about football and prayed."

Such was the manner in which Craig Morton, swinging man-about-Dallas, spent his time following one of his early heroic performances as a professional quarterback. Not in Aspen or at Ruidoso or dancing the night away in one of Dallas' tinseled discotheques but, rather, in the quiet hospital room of a dying little boy.

It was a side of Craig Morton few knew in those days.

He was twenty-six then, an athlete whose past had been impressive but whose future loomed even more promising. As a schoolboy in Campbell, California, Morton had earned All-State honors in football, basketball, and baseball. At the University of California he had been a consensus All-American and was among the top vote-getters in the balloting for the 1964 Heisman Trophy. Major league baseball scouts offered impressive bonuses if he would pursue their sport, but when the Cowboys selected him in the first round of the 1965 draft, his athletic future was charted.

In his early years with the Cowboys he would learn the complicated Tom Landry offensive system while serving as an apprentice to Meredith. While he played sparingly, he regularly drew praise for his ability. Clearly, he was Dallas' quarterback of the future and was content to wait patiently for his time to come.

He was on a fishing trip, camped beside the Russian River in northern California when Meredith announced his retirement plans. "I was," Morton remembers, "driving back to San Francisco and heard it on the radio. The fact that Don had decided to retire really didn't surprise me all that much. The miracle was that there wasn't a whole string of wrecks along the highway after I heard the news."

Those fickle Dallas fans who had been, for the past few seasons, booing Meredith and chanting, "We want Morton," were certain that his ascent to the No. 1 job would at last put to rest the myth that the Cowboys couldn't win the big ones.

Because of his lengthy tenure as the backup quarterback, Morton was able to make the transition to full-time duty with ease. Enroute to directing Dallas to a 11–2–1 season he performed solidly, often brilliantly, despite laboring under the handicap of a separated right shoulder much of the year.

On a dismal Sunday in October he had suffered the injury against Atlanta and there was serious doubt that he would be able to play the following week against the Philadelphia Eagles. In fact, the 71,509 who turned out in the Cotton Bowl had been made aware throughout the week that Morton would probably view the contest from a sideline vantage point. He had not thrown at all during the week's practice and reportedly was still suffering considerable pain.

"The day of the game was warm though," recalls Morton, "so I decided to give it a try during pregame warmups and see if I could throw. I got a shot in the shoulder to numb the pain and started warming up. After a while Coach Landry came over and asked me what I thought and I told him I'd give it a try."

Suffice it to say it was not a totally confident Craig Morton who went out on the field for the first series of offensive downs. "Shoot, I was as much in the dark about how I would be able to perform as anyone," he says, "but Landry had told me he would leave the final decision up to me and I had made it, so I was determined to have a go at it. I remember being aware of the pain in the shoulder even though the medication I had taken was supposed to have taken care of it."

To avoid the suspense of an O. Henry ending to this anecdote, be aware that on that sunny Sunday afternoon as Dallas defeated the Eagles 49–14, Morton hit 13 of 19 passing attempts for 247 yards and 5 touchdowns. The performance tied a club record set originally by Eddie LeBaron in 1962 and equalled by Meredith on three occasions.

"It was one of those days," Morton remembers, "when everything just seemed to go right. The blocking was great, the receivers were getting open, and I was on the money. The better things got, the better the shoulder felt. By the time the game was over I had completely forgotten the pain."

Though briefly forgotten, the pain would remain for the rest of the season. In an attempt to compensate for the shoulder injury, Morton altered his throwing style, trying a sidearm delivery which would eventually damage his elbow. By the time Dallas faced Cleveland in the Eastern Division championship game, Morton's passing was erratic, often ineffective.

The Browns trounced the Cowboys 38–14 and Morton prepared for off-season surgery.

While not fully recovered, Morton would have his moments the following season as he led the Cowboys to the Super Bowl for the first time in the club's history. Along the way he would equal his touchdown performance of the previous year, throwing 5 scoring passes against Houston. On that particular Sunday he would complete 13 of 17 attempts for 349 yards. The superlative performances, however, were often matched by days when his passes were far off target and the potent Dallas offense made little noise. By the end of the season, in fact, it was the Cowboys' defense which kept the drive to the Super Bowl alive as Dallas clinched the Eastern title with a 6–2 win over Cleveland and defeated Detroit 5–0 in the Divisional title game.

By the time the Cowboys prepared to face Baltimore in Super Bowl V, the national media was calling it a team with little chance and referring to Morton as the worst quarterback ever to make it to pro football's biggest game. The Colts won 16–13 on a last-minute field goal by Jim O'Brien and the Dallas fans began to grumble.

They were looking for a new champion to cheer. Now it was Morton being booed and a young retired Navy officer named Roger Staubach whom they were chanting for. When Dallas reported to training camp in Thousand Oaks, California, to begin preparations for the '71 season, Tom Landry made it clear that the quarterbacking job was up for grabs.

Morton's spiralling career was beginning to slide. The next three seasons would be a never ending struggle. First, Landry alternated Morton and Staubach, then he turned the job over to the former Heisman Trophy winner from Navy. Staubach responded by leading Dallas to a 24–3 victory over the Miami Dolphins in Super Bowl VI.

Craig Morton's days in Dallas were numbered. Many felt his career had reached its climax. Not satisfied as a backup quarterback after ten years' tenure, he asked to be traded and was dealt to the New York Giants midway through the 1974 season.

In his two and one-half years with the Giants he completed 461 passes for 5,734 yards and 29 touchdowns but failed to turn the once-proud New York team into a winner. The boos were louder than they had ever been in Dallas. New York began shopping for another quarterback.

The Denver Broncos offered to exchange Steve Ramsey for the thirteen-year veteran. To most close followers of the NFL wars it appeared that Denver, with an impressive roster of young and gifted quarterbacks, needed a veteran to step in and take the hard knocks for awhile as the youngsters learned the system.

Craig Morton viewed his role differently.

At age thirty-four he was eager for yet another shot at the brass ring, for a chance to prove himself the caliber quarterback he remained certain he was—or could be. Craig Morton's competitive edge had not dulled during the up-and-down years preceding his late arrival in Denver.

Other things, however, had changed. Wearied of the bright lights and the swinging bachelor life style, he had gone in search of something to fill a void he had begun to feel in his life. At the urging of girl friend Susie Sirmen, a Dallas model and reborn Christian, Morton began to read the Bible seriously.

Reporting to the Broncos camp in the best condition

of his life, Morton dedicated himself to two things: Christ and becoming the starting quarterback for the new team which had employed him.

"I realized finally that I had wasted a lot of years," he said. "Up until the time I fully accepted Christ my life had been fairly easy to sketch. I was a free spirit who would do things on the spur of the moment. I was a bachelor with a nice apartment and a lot of things which really had no value attached to them. My life was sporadic, and my football playing was, too. Christ was trying to get my attention but for a lot of reasons I simply wasn't aware of it."

From the outset it was obvious that the 1977 Denver Broncos season would not be wasted. With Morton as the catalyst, the Broncos got off to a furious start and never slowed. The long standing also-rans suddenly were not ready to accept their annual defeats from the Oaklands and the Pittsburghs. Nor would they submit to those midseason lulls that had, in the past, caused them to lose an occasional game they were supposed to win. As Sunday success piled upon Sunday success, the city of Denver would bring a new word to the English language: Broncomania. They painted street signs orange, the color of the uniforms worn by their heroes. They were the first believers. This, they sensed, was not the Cinderella team many writers were leading their readers to believe. It was a solid, talented, and courageous football team destined for the American Football Conference title and a spot in the Super Bowl.

And the man piloting the drive was Craig Morton. In a matter of a few short months, he became the city's favorite son. In fact, when he flew into Dallas in midseason to marry Susie Sirmen, the newlyweds returned to Denver to find the driveway of their newly rented home carpeted in red and a large trophy reading "Champions" on the lawn.

Morton went out the following Sunday and lived up to the engraving on the trophy.

Only a loss to defending Super Bowl champion Oakland stood between Denver and a perfect record when it traveled to Dallas for the final regular season game against the Cowboys. In an attempt to hype the game, some writers called it a preview of the Super Bowl.

With the playoffs ahead and the division title already won, Denver coach Red Miller wasn't interested in doing much previewing. While many on hand in Texas Stadium were there to witness a matchup not of Denver and Dallas but, instead, of Morton and Staubach, Miller chose to play his starting quarterback but one series of downs. Dallas won and the sportswriters howled.

Miller then revealed that Morton, having played for several weeks with a badly bruised hip, had spent the days prior to the Cowboys encounter in the hospital. "There is too much at stake to risk further injury to the man who is most responsible for our being in the playoffs," Miller said.

He stopped short of promising that Dallas fans would get another chance to witness a Morton-Staubach battle. First, the Broncos would have to defeat Pittsburgh and Oakland (the team favored by most to represent the AFC in New Orleans and one Denver had split with in the regular season) in the playoffs.

A numbing north wind had thundered into New Orleans as literally hundreds of the nation's newsmen gathered for the pandemonium that is known as Super Bowl XII Press Day. On the field of ancient Tulane Stadium, just a few miles removed from the massive

Superdome where the Super Bowl would be played, television cameras hummed and questions interrupted questions as Craig Morton held court beneath one of the goal posts.

Members of the media wanted to know how it felt to be facing his old team in pro football's biggest game. ("I have a lot of friends on the Cowboys," he said, "but the main thing I'll be looking at is a lot of blank faces on the other side of the line.") They wanted to know how recent word that the Internal Revenue Service had revealed a serious tax deficiency in Morton's personal accounting would affect his mental preparation for the biggest game of his life. ("It's being taken care of," he replied, "and that's all I'm going to say about it.") And they wanted to know more about his religious conversion.

He answered eagerly and personally.

"That's one thing I like to talk about," he said. "I'm very proud of the fact that I'm a Christian. I came to accept the Lord through my wife and it is, by far, the greatest thing that has ever happened to me. From the time I said, 'Lord, my life is in your hands. I have no conditions. Whatever you will, I'll do,' everything has been wonderful. I'm not talking about just football and our being here in the Super Bowl. I mean everything."

He told of the Bible study which numerous members of the Broncos attend each Sunday morning prior to games and of the monthly potluck suppers they have. "This fall," he said, "we studied the Book of Acts and learned a great deal about the formation of the early churches and what the early Christians had to go through."

"There are a lot of dedicated Christians on our team," he continued, "but when you go into our dressing room you're going to see just as much horseplay and fun as any other. The difference is a sense of closeness, a genuine concern for each other as human beings, not just as football players."

And he spoke of the upcoming game; of his belief that the underdog Denver Broncos, the team few thought would ever make it to the Super Bowl, had a very real chance of defeating the Cowboys.

It was not to be. Under a constant, devastating pressure from the Dallas defense, Morton had thrown for four interceptions in the first half—a Super Bowl record —and was replaced by backup quarterback Norris Weese. For the second time in his career, Morton had made it to the Super Bowl and not realized the thrill of victory.

Once again, after the Cowboys had scored a decisive 27–10 win. Morton was besieged by writers in the postgame locker room. Unlike many before him who had endured troubled days and then slipped away to the privacy of a too-long shower to escape the pointed questions, Morton accepted his fate with dignity and class.

"It was," he said, "a bad time to play a bad game— and I played a bad game. Naturally, I'm disappointed that we didn't win. That's what we were here for; what we wanted to do. But I'm not as dejected as many of you probably expect me to be. A lot of wonderful things have happened to me—and to this team—this year. Nobody even expected us to be here. I'm proud the Lord got us this far. What we'll have to do now is just start over next year."

Later, after the journalists had retreated in search of the Roger Staubachs, the Tony Dorsetts, and the Harvey Martins, heroes of the day, Andy Maurer, the standout offensive tackle of the Broncos, approached the solemn-faced Morton. He stood, towering over his quarterback for a moment, and then broke into a smile. He hugged him and said, "Craig, thanks for getting me here."

Now Morton smiled. And began to dress. Even in defeat he seemed relaxed, at peace. A new season would be beginning in just a few months. He was confident it would be a good one.

TERRY BRADSHAW

Quarterback, Pittsburgh Steelers

IT WAS THE FINAL Tuesday morning of January, 1970, and Art Rooney, Jr., personnel director for the Pittsburgh Steelers football team (which his then sixty-eight-year-old father owned), sat in his office, glancing first at his watch, then at the list of names written on a nearby blackboard.

The time had come for the National Football League teams to make their annual college draft selections. At exactly 10 A.M. the Steelers' representative in attendance at the draft meeting being held in the ballroom of New York's Belmont Plaza Hotel was to place a call to Rooney in Pittsburgh for the final decision on who would be the Steelers' first pick.

Waiting for the phone to ring, Rooney had already come to a decision. The call came, he spoke briefly to the anxious man in New York, then replaced the receiver and smiled.

At the Belmont Plaza word was hurried to NFL commissioner Pete Rozelle who in turn went before a maze of television cameras and microphones and anxious sportswriters. He cleared his voice, made a dramatic pause, and said:

"Pittsburgh . . . First choice in the first round . . . Terry Bradshaw, quarterback from Louisiana Tech. . . ."

Down in Ruston, Louisiana, a 6'-2½", 215-pound youngster (numerous professional scouts had said he could throw the ball like the legendary Sammy Baugh, a country boy quarterback from another time in sports history) became an instant celebrity: interviews with members of the press from coast-to-coast, featured on the cover of *Newsweek* and *Sports Illustrated* magazines, posing for a men's fashion layout in *Vogue,* constant requests for autographs. He was a pro football star before ever reporting to his first preseason training camp. Art Rooney himself proudly pointed to the big blond youngster and insisted this was the individual who would lead the stumbling, struggling Steelers from the ranks of the downtrodden underdogs.

"Give him five years," said father Bill Bradshaw, "and Terry will have Pittsburgh in the Super Bowl." Steeler fans, convinced that the local team would have to show miraclelike improvement to win even two straight hands of gin rummy, found themselves believing all the things they were hearing and reading. This talented rookie seemed almost too good to be real: strong arm, All-American credentials, leadership ability, and a God-fearing young man not at all shy about voicing his Christian conviction.

In one of his first press conferences he had spoken enthusiastically of his Christian faith, of his strict Baptist upbringing, of his summers spent speaking at church and youth rallies, of his interest in working in the Fellowship of Christian Athletes.

"I'm no saint," he pointed out, "but I have a strong feeling about doing the best I can to live a Christian life. But I'm aware that athletes don't have any inside track with God so I have to work just as hard at being a Christian as the next fellow."

His country drawl sincerity came through loud and clear. Pittsburgh fans welcomed Terry Bradshaw with open arms. He was the toast of the town before he even found an apartment.

That's how it was in the early days of his life as a pro football player. The Cinderella world of a young back-woods boy who seemed to be ripped from the pages of a Jack Armstrong novel captured the fancy of the football-crazed American sports world.

That was in the early days.

Go now to the 1974 season. Terry Bradshaw was sitting on the Pittsburgh bench, watching as an unheralded Jim Gilliam performed as the No. 1 Steelers quarterback. Head coach Chuck Noll was down on the benched player who had been the starting quarterback since his rookie season. The frustrated Pittsburgh fans, having seen just enough of the Steelers winning to develop a strong taste for it, were down on Bradshaw. And Bradshaw was down on Bradshaw. There were also bitter words from the sportswriters assigned to cover the Steelers. Many who had written glowing descriptions of the Louisiana youngster a few years earlier had come to the conclusion that neither Pittsburgh nor Bradshaw were ever going to be big winners—particularly as long as they were partners in crime.

Bradshaw's problem, they had decided, was simply that he was dumb. Not only did he bear physical resemblance to the comic strip character Lil Abner, he seemed to have the same I.Q. displayed by the Dogpatch dimwit. Super Bowls are not won, it was repeatedly pointed out, with dummies at the controls.

The Cinderella story had come to an end. Midnight had come and gone. And Bradshaw sat on the bench, disillusioned, confused, bitter, and making noises about being traded.

"It was," he says in retrospect, "a low point in my life. I just couldn't understand what was happening to me. I had some personal problems that I was struggling with (he and his wife Melissa had divorced after the 1973 season) and I just wasn't performing on the football field. My confidence was just about nonexistent."

The pressure of trying to live up to an overgrown advance build-up had gradually taken its toll. The four-year quest for the greatness everyone expected had seemingly ended with Bradshaw sitting on the sideline, relegated to the role of back-up punter—a well-paid, highly publicized failure.

In his much ballyhooed rookie year his statistics had been less than superlative. He had completed only 83 passes in 218 tries for a 38.1 percentage. NFL secondaries had a field day week after week, picking off 24 of his passes.

There was some sign of improvement in 1971 as his

completion percentage rose to 50 and he threw 13 touch-down passes. But the interception plague continued to haunt him. Defenders picked off 22 of his passes.

The two years that followed were similarly average. He continued to complete about half his passes but the Steelers began to depend more and more on a running attack built around newcomer Franco Harris and a vastly improved defense led by Joe Greene, L. C. Greenwood, and Jack Ham. No longer was Bradshaw the top attraction.

There were those, in fact, who insisted that the Steelers had progressed to a point in their development where they had begun to win in spite of Bradshaw rather than because of him. In 1972 and 1973 the Pittsburgh Steelers, of all people, advanced to the playoffs. But as team fortunes were on the rise, Bradshaw was going in the opposite direction. In 1974 he reached new depths and the Steelers slid back into the role of also-ran.

Then came the roller-coaster 1975 season, one which would include the low and high points of Bradshaw's career up to that time.

It began with an arm injury midway through the pre-season schedule, sidelining him for two weeks. Gilliam stepped into the quarterbacking job and his passing proved to be everything people had initially expected from Bradshaw. In the regular season the Steelers won four, tied one, and lost one in their first six appearances. There was little spark, few signs of polish or daring, but they were winning again.

The season was seven games old before Bradshaw got his first start. He was sharp against Atlanta, leading his team to an easy victory. But the next week he was inept against Cincinnati. It was the first sign of a pattern that would develop. Against New Orleans he was outstanding, hitting his receivers, selecting plays, running with the ball. Six days later against Houston he was almost booed off the field. It was decision time for Pittsburgh coach Noll.

He announced to a rather surprised press luncheon the Monday following the Houston disaster that Terry Bradshaw would be his starting quarterback the following Sunday against the New England Patriots. It was an announcement which would reopen the door to stardom for Terry Bradshaw.

"When Noll showed that he had faith in me even after the way I had played against Houston, everything began to come together for me. Even before that I believe I had gone a long way toward solving my problems. It had occurred to me that I had lost faith not only in myself but in God as well. I knew that was wrong, a foolish thing for me to do, so I returned to my faith in him and the Bible. I had suddenly realized that I needed help— not so much as a football player but as a person—and I knew that God was the place I could get it. I don't mean I prayed to him to help me read zone defenses better. I just asked him to help me get my life back together, to help me be the best person I could be. I read the Bible and prayed, trying to get my head straight and fight through the depression that I had allowed myself to fall into," Bradshaw remembers.

His performance against New England was to be the first of five straight games which would border on perfection. "I never questioned my abilities from then on," he says. "I felt in those few weeks that I proved I could make it as a professional quarterback."

The ranks of the anti-Bradshaw fans began to go their fickle way. Talk of Bradshaw's intellectual capabilities was replaced with praise for his direction of the Steelers' offense which had suddenly bloomed into the finest in the NFL.

In Pittsburgh's 32–14 playoff-opening victory over Buffalo, he made three first downs rushing on third and fourth downs to keep crucial first half drives alive which eventually accounted for the ten decisive points. A week later in Oakland it was his six-yard touchdown pass to then rookie wide receiver Lynn Swann which sewed up a 24–13 victory.

Despite his ups and downs, Terry Bradshaw was right on the schedule his father had predicted. The Steelers were in the Super Bowl with the chance of providing owner Art Rooney with his first NFL championship in forty years.

As they prepared to square off against the Minnesota Vikings, Bradshaw, his confidence again intact and his sense of humor returned, would not be ruffled by even the most pointed questions thrown at him by the multitude of writers on hand in New Orleans to cover Super Bowl IX.

"You've got a reputation for being a dumb quarterback," one said. "How smart are you?"

Six months earlier Bradshaw would have handled the point blank question differently. Like with no answer. Or maybe by poking the insensitive journalist in the nose. But now Terry just grinned.

"Well," he said, "I'm just barely smart enough to get Pittsburgh in the Super Bowl." He had won his first victory of the Super Bowl.

The tension gone, he settled back and spoke freely with the reporters. "I know some of you are wondering how smart I am," he said. "Well, I did graduate from high school, I got my Bachelor of Arts degree from

Louisiana Tech with an average that put me in the middle of my class. Personally, I don't think that makes me dumb." End of intellectual discussion. Terry Bradshaw was in New Orleans to play a football game, not defend his I.Q.

There would be skeptics right up to the Sunday kick-off, of course. The twenty-six-year-old Bradshaw needed only three hours to win them over.

The favored Vikings, piloted by the much applauded Fran Tarkenton, were no match for the Steelers. It would not be a day of long-bomb completions or breath-taking runs for Bradshaw, nor would it be an afternoon when any last-minute heroics would be necessary.

In fact, the spotlight would shine on the powerful running of Harris and the brilliant play of the Steeler defense. But throughout the afternoon it was Bradshaw's near perfect play calling which set the Steeler ground game on its way. For icing on the 16–6 victory, he rifled a touchdown pass to tight end Larry Brown late in the fourth quarter which would make the frustrated Vikings the first three-time loser in the nine-year history of the Super Bowl.

In the dressing room there was the expected amount of celebrating, cheering, congratulating, and instant replay reflection on the championship the Steelers had just claimed. Almost to a man the members of the Steelers team filed by Bradshaw's locker to extend a handshake or a slap on the back. There was little question that he was once again the leader of the squad.

It would be defensive standout Joe Greene who would perhaps best sum up the situation: "What happened to us during the last few weeks of the regular season and even more so in the playoffs," he said, "was that Terry Bradshaw matured as a man. Oh, he matured as a quarter-back, too, don't get me wrong, but maturing as a man is much more important."

Across the way in the somber Vikings dressing room Minnesota defender Alan Page gave credit to Bradshaw. "I guess we fell for that dumb quarterback stuff. We thought we could rattle him, get him to make that one big mistake, and then fall apart. We sacked him the first two times he tried to throw and thought maybe he would begin to feel the pressure. But he never flinched. He went to work on us real good, as good or better than any quarterback we've faced. If Terry Bradshaw is dumb then I'm a Las Vegas fan dancer."

There is no one alive who could confuse the hulking All-Pro Page with a Vegas fan dancer.

And so, at age twenty-six, five years deep into his professional football career, Bradshaw had climbed to the highest perch the game has to offer. He had quarter-backed his team to victory in the Super Bowl. Terry Bradshaw had come a long way.

A long way from those afternoons back in Shreveport when, as a second grader he got his first taste of organized football as a seventy-five pound offensive guard on a local Pop Warner team. "My career," he is fond of saying, "got off and running with all the promise of a busted play."

Indeed, he would have to convince people of his abilities long before signing a Pittsburgh contract.

Even before entering junior high he had known what his goal was, that he wanted to quarterback a pro team one day, but the road would not be easy. As a seventh grader he was small and skinny and the football coaches were selecting only big boys for their team. Terry was not among those issued a uniform. In the eighth grade the same thing happened. He attended the first meeting of team prospects and again was told he was too small, too frail. This time, however, the coach left a crack in the door. Those not picked for the team were welcome to come watch practices if they so wished.

Already confident in his ability as a passer, Bradshaw reported to the sidelines faithfully, determined to show that he deserved a spot on the team. When he noticed a coach looking his way he would immediately pick up a football and begin throwing beautiful spiraling passes to another youngster who had failed to make the team. One afternoon his performance managed to hold the coach's attention longer than usual. "For the next ten minutes I did everything I knew how to do with a foot-ball—and some I didn't. I threw short, long, on the run. I ran to my right and threw to my left. Ran to my left and threw to my right, every time throwing the ball just as far as I could."

Thus Terry Bradshaw, sideline-passing wizard, made the team—as a middle linebacker. And broke his collar-bone twice that season.

It was not until he entered high school that he had a chance to play the position he wanted. But once settled into the job of quarterbacking he proved his worth. In his senior year he led Shreveport's Woodlawn High into the Louisiana state playoffs in what local sportswriters had felt would be a rebuilding year for the team. In the battle for the state championship, Bradshaw was unable to display the passing which had earned him a spreading reputation in Louisiana prep circles. The game was played in a driving rain and Woodlawn lost, 12–9.

But Bradshaw had established himself as a prime college prospect. Recruiters from throughout the southwest came to visit him. He traveled to LSU to visit the Baton Rouge campus. He went to look over the facilities at Baylor. And when he wasn't trying to decide on which football scholarship to accept he was busy throwing the javelin for the track team. In his senior year he set a national schoolboy record with a throw of 243 feet, 7 inches. Offers of track scholarships poured in from almost 150 schools. Bradshaw was first and foremost a football player, however, a quarterback. College ball would be the next step toward the realization of his dream. Much to the surprise of many who assumed he would cast his lot with one of the "big name" football powers, he accepted an offer to attend Louisiana Tech. The reason for his choice was simple. Tech ran a wide-open pro-style offense with the quarterback expected to throw the ball a great deal.

By the end of his junior year he had led the nation in passing and in total yardage, throwing as many as fifty passes in a single game. By the end of his senior year he was being touted as the best pro quarterback prospect in the country. Terry Bradshaw had come a long way even before he became a pro, before he led his team to the Super Bowl championship.

And there is now reason to believe that Bradshaw, his days of having to prove himself finally behind him, may well continue to climb, to improve, fullfilling those signing day promises. Already he has accomplished what few quarterbacks in the pro game's history have done. In Super Bowl X against the Dallas Cowboys he led Pittsburgh to a second consecutive championship.

In his second Super Bowl appearance Bradshaw was even more impressive than he had been a year earlier against Minnesota. This time there were precious few questions about his academic background or his latest aptitude test. He completed 9 of 19 passes for 202 yards and 2 touchdowns to bring the Steelers from a 10–7 half-time deficit to a 21–17 victory. His final effort of the day, a high, arching, perfectly timed 64-yard touchdown bomb to Swann iced the victory—and sent him to the dressing room in the waning minutes of the game, kayoed by the blitzing Dallas defense. Terry Bradshaw did not see the winning pass completed. Until after the game was over he did not even know it had resulted in a Steelers touchdown which would earn him and his teammates a second championship.

He did not see it but the rest of the football world did. Terry Bradshaw had again proved himself. On this particular occasion, however, it had not really been all that necessary.

Bradshaw is now married to the former JoJo Starbuck, a figure skater for the U. S. in the 1972 Olympics and Ice Capades star. They spend their off-season each year on their 400-acre cattle ranch in Grand Cane, Louisiana.

KYLE ROTE, JR.

Superstars Champion (Soccer)

THE YEAR WAS 1974 and already it had been one of satisfying accomplishment for a young man whose name was considerably better known to the American sports public than the game he played. Kyle Rote, Jr., son of the legendary New York Giants halfback, had chosen to focus his athletic attention on professional soccer. In his first season with the Dallas Tornado of the North American Soccer League he had been named Rookie of the Year and had won the scoring title.

Yet outside of the still modest number of Americans who were taking an interest in the sport which enjoys fanatical popularity in over 140 countries throughout the world, the boyish-looking young Texan could hardly be considered a full-blown celebrity. The fact that he had become the first native American to lead all NASL scorers (10 goals and 10 assists) caused no great rush of manufacturers to seek his endorsement of their products. No movie directors offered cameo parts to the twenty-three-year-old center-forward, a bubble gum card bearing his picture was not to be found, and Johnny Carson was yet to call. In fact, his annual salary of $1,400 would have caused major league baseball players, NBA benchwarmers, and pro football rookies to question his status as a professional athlete.

Then came a call from the promotion department of ABC-TV, inviting the new sport's newest star to join a stellar collection of the nation's professional athletes to compete in a decathlon-type event called the Superstars Competition. Designed as a television showcase of great athletes, its purpose was to lure a large number of the country's sports fans to sit and watch as men like NFL Player of the Year O. J. Simpson, Boston Celtics All-Pro John Havlicek, baseball's Pete Rose, hockey's Stan Mikita, tennis' Stan Smith, and auto racing's Peter Revson, to name a few, did battle in a ten-event program.

In all, forty-eight participants would be asked to compete in four qualifying rounds with the top twelve advancing to the two-day grand finale which would be served up on national television. To round out the field and add the spice of a possible darkhorse entry here and there, ABC decided to invite representatives from such stepchild sports as speed skating, skiing, track and field, and soccer. It was decided that the six-foot, 180-pound Rote could best fly the banner of the North American Soccer League.

Few gave him a chance to seriously challenge the big names of American sport. Yet Kyle Rote, Jr., needed no prolonged thought to accept the invitation and immediately set about to prepare himself for the unique competition.

On the program would be 10 events—a 100-yard dash, 880-yard run, 100-meter swim, tennis, baseball hitting, golf, bowling, a one-mile cycle race, tennis, and an obstacle course. Each competitor could choose seven events to compete in but would be prohibited from choosing an event which coincided with the sport in which he earned his living. For instance, baseball star Reggie Jackson would not be allowed to compete in the baseball hitting, and naturally Stan Smith would be prohibited from entering the tennis competition. A complex point system, giving 10 points for first, 7 for second, and so on, would eventually determine the overall winner.

Rote set about to prepare himself in a manner some would term obsessive. No sooner had the invitation been extended to him than he decided he would take full advantage of the opportunity given him. "The idea of being able to compete against some of the greatest athletes in the world," he told his wife Mary Lynne, "is an exciting challenge. If I can do well, it could help focus some attention on professional soccer, and we both know that the money would come in handy." To a young bride attempting to set up housekeeping on a pro soccer player's salary, the thousands of dollars being offered the winner of the

Superstar Competition looked like the pot of gold at the end of the rainbow.

For eight back-breaking weeks, Kyle worked toward the first round of the competition. He had not even owned a tennis racket but soon got one and was taking lessons daily at the famed T-Bar-N tennis club. He rented a couple of bicycles and he and his wife decided to forego any other form of transportation for the weeks to come, riding to the store, to visit friends, to church, and to classes where Rote was completing his first semester at Dallas' Perkins School of Theology.

He joined the YMCA and worked out daily in the pool, strengthening himself for the 100-meter swim event. At a nearby bowling alley he bowled over 100 games. A friend who was a golf pro at a Dallas country club volunteered to give lessons to the young competitor whose only equipment was a starter set of clubs his parents had given him when he was twelve years old.

Always one to set high goals for himself, Kyle Rote, Jr., went quietly and feverishly about his task of transforming himself into an all-round athlete.

The work paid off when he won in the first round of competition, beating such better known athletes as tennis great Rod Laver and baseball standouts Reggie Jackson and Jim Palmer.

At the mid-February finals in Rotonda, Rote wasted little time making his presence known. In the opening day of competition he defeated Simpson, 6–4, Havlicek, 6–3, and basketball standout Jim McMillan, 6–4, to finish first in the tennis. That accomplished, he rushed out to the golf course where he shot a respectable 43 for nine holes. That total would be good enough for second place behind the 41 of Miami Dolphins safety Dick Anderson and better than the efforts of such name athletes as Pittsburgh

Steeler running back Franco Harris, Pete Rose, and Stan Smith.

Later in the afternoon, facing defending champion Bob Seagren, Olympic pole vault champion and a member of the newly formed pro track tour, the determined young soccer player scored an arm's length victory in the 100-meter swim. Later that evening, tired but eager to improve his point total, he defeated shot-putter Brian Oldfield by 48 pins to take first place in the bowling.

With four events behind him, Rote held a commanding lead and was suddenly signing as many autographs and granting more interviews than the well-known athletes he was competing against.

On the second day he failed to place in the baseball hitting, an event he had won in the qualifying round, and was next to last in the grueling 880-yard run. But in the cycle race he finished a strong second to Holland speed skater Ard Schenk. For the seven events he had chosen to participate in Rote had amassed 44 points. His closest challenger, Seagren, accumulated 38.

For his efforts Kyle Rote, Jr., received a check for $53,000 dollars and a trophy signifying him as the Superstar of the Year. Suddenly he was no longer just another face in the crowded world of professional sport.

In the span of the nationally televised event, the sports-crazed American public had found itself a new hero; one who ranked as something of a throwback to the all-but-forgotten Chip Hilton days. Here was an almost shy divinity student soundly defeating high-salaried, well-publicized competitors from a pro sports world where the swinging life style is commonplace and the Big Buck is life's brass ring.

In the aftermath of his victory he would tell reporters that having been able to compete against athletes he had heard so much and read so much about for most of his life was one of the greatest thrills he had ever experienced. And what, they had wanted to know, was he going to do with his new-found wealth? "Life has been good to me," he explained, "so I have no intention of keeping all of the money. I plan to share it with people who need it. To be honest, I've never worried much about having a lot of money."

With that he packed his trophy and headed back to Dallas to the $85-a-month apartment he and his wife called home.

His athletic career began as one might expect of a youngster with a famous football-playing father. It had been on the campus of Southern Methodist, just a few blocks from the Rote home, where Kyle, Sr. had earned All-American honors.

Kyle, Jr., everyone felt, was destined to follow in his dad's footsteps. As a senior at Highland Park High, a school whose football tradition is dotted with the names of such alumni as Doak Walker and Bobby Layne, Kyle Rote, Jr., was the team's leader, an All-State quarterback and defensive safety in his senior year. No fewer than fifty colleges offered scholarships to the gifted youngster who had also captained the basketball and baseball teams.

And as a teenager his goals weren't much different from those of most high school athletes in the state of Texas. "One day," he would say, "I would like to be good enough to play professional football. That is the goal I set for myself back when I first started playing."

It was one he would carry on to Oklahoma State University with him where his football career would be short-circuited after only two months as a collegian. During a freshman team workout he suffered a broken leg.

As he worked to rehabilitate the leg, isolated from the

daily competition of workouts and games, young Rote began to take stock of his station in life. The atmosphere of big-time college athletics, he found, was not designed to help a struggling freshman with less than ideal study habits along the road to academic success. The athletes were housed in their own dorm, separated from the rest of the campus. He began to question the course he had chosen.

And with time on his hands he found himself thinking back to the summers before when, in an effort to keep himself in condition, he had joined some of his friends in games of sandlot soccer back in Dallas. The more he had played the game and learned about it, the more he liked it. Soccer offered a challenge he could not totally understand or explain. All he knew was that he liked it and wanted to play more of it.

"I had so much fun playing soccer," he says, "that I wanted to become more involved in it. And it occurred to me that I was missing out on a lot of other things, being so involved in football and little else in college. I knew I didn't have the self-discipline to take care of my studies the way I should with all the activity that goes on in a college athletic dorm. In that kind of atmosphere it takes a very dedicated person to keep his priorities in the proper order."

At the end of his freshman year he transferred to the University of the South at Sewanee, Tennessee, giving up a full athletic scholarship to pay his own way. He spent his energies on his studies and his leisure time joining other nonscholarship athletes on the school soccer team.

"A lot of people think it a little strange," Kyle says, "but my dad had as much to do with my decision to transfer as anyone. When I was growing up he had frequently made it clear that he always needed an escape from football. We had a cottage on Long Island when we lived in New York where he liked to go to write poetry and to paint. He was always telling me how important it was to have a vocation outside of football because football might not last that long. He made me aware that there were other things more important than sports.

"Actually, I did miss football for a while after I transferred but as time went along I just found soccer to be more enjoyable."

Rote switched his major from engineering to psychology, enjoyed a variety of campus involvements, and the day after his 1972 graduation married a pretty sophomore from Georgia named Mary Lynne Lykins in the Sewanee chapel.

Another event transpired during the whirlwind days of his final spring at the 991-student school which would alter his life considerably. Rote was casually aware of the North American Soccer League, an attempt to add yet another sport to the nation's professional sports community. With teams composed almost entirely of transplanted European soccer players, the league had, in one form or another, been in existence since 1967, receiving a mild reception from the public and the media alike.

Rote, then, was surprised to learn that the Dallas Tornado, the franchise in his hometown which was owned by millionaire Lamar Hunt, had selected him as its number one draft choice that year. "I was tickled to death about it," Rote recalls, "but to be quite honest I wasn't even aware that they had a draft until I was selected."

The newlyweds returned to Dallas, set up housekeeping in a small apartment, and Rote began pursuit of yet another athletic goal: that of becoming a professional soccer player.

It was widely felt that Dallas' purpose in drafting the young Sewanee graduate was based more on publicity and promotional promise than in the player's abilities to compete with veterans from abroad who had played the game all their lives.

"The first time I saw him," said Tornado coach Ron Newman, "he didn't look too polished. He was big and strong and eager to learn. But outside of those qualities there wasn't too much to indicate he was going to become one of the league's top players."

Aware of the critical eye with which his every move as a professional would be watched, Rote sought help and advice from his teammates and spent long hours on the practice field after other members of the Tornado had retreated to the showers.

His home debut came in Texas Stadium against the Toronto Metros with a crowd of 19,342 in the stands despite a day-long deluge. Rote did not disappoint them. In a 2–1 Tornado victory he headed home the first goal and it was his intimidating presence which helped set up the winning goal scored by teammate John Collins.

After the game Tornado defender John Best, an all-leaguer from Liverpool, said, "The feeling of the players might once have been that Kyle was here because of his name and the fact he is American. Now it is believed that he is here (in the NASL) because he has earned the right."

Rote worked hard to earn that place. When he wasn't practicing at the field, he was seeking the help of his new bride at home. Mary Lynne would throw balls at him from various angles and shag for him in a nearby park. "Kyle," she would observe, "is a fierce competitor. He hates to lose at anything. I've never known anyone who works as hard as he does at whatever he sets his mind to do."

No doubt this was one of the primary reasons for his steady program which would ultimately earn him Rookie of the Year honors—and his first invitation to the Superstars competition.

Since that time the young Rote's life has been a swirl of public appearances, recognition, and steady improvement as a soccer player. Twice Dallas has captured division titles and in Kyle's initial season went to the NASL Championships before losing 2–0 to Philadelphia. It had been Rote's goal which had enabled Dallas to score a 1–0 win over New York in the semifinals.

And even as his excellence as a soccer player would be gradually recognized, it has been the annual Superstars competition which has earned him the greatest athletic recognition. Following his initial victory in 1974, he would win the title again in 1976 and 1977 and to date can count $187,825 earned from the Superstars events alone.

The Rotes now live in an old two-story brick home in a picturesque section of Dallas, restoring it to their own taste. Outside of New York's famed Pele, now retired, Kyle has for the past several years been the best-known soccer player in America. By all measures applied in today's sports world, he is a thundering success.

All of which has done little to change his life style or his thinking. He still looks toward graduation from the Perkins School of Theology as the next big step in his life.

"It's something that has been on my mind for several years now," he says. "All of these things that I've been fortunate enough to have happen to me in sports are just preliminary to doing the work of God. I'm trying to do that work right now, in my role as an athlete, because an athlete has a tremendous opportunity to influence young people. And with that opportunity comes a great responsibility. I pray every night that the inroads I have gained can be used to good purpose."

And even as his status as a soccer star continues to rise, Rote insists that he would not be greatly affected if his career came to an end today. "I love the game," he says, "and the association with teammates and friends which it has brought to me. But there is far more to life than just soccer. I want to look ahead to a lot of new and different things. I certainly don't gauge my self-worth just by how I do as a soccer player."

When he first entered the Perkins School of Theology, Rote's goal was eventual ordination as an Episcopalian priest. But soccer success and Superstars triumphs have given him a broader, more wide-ranging base from which to share his convictions. "I'm beginning to think," he says, "that I might be able to have a greater influence if I don't put on a collar. Sports has given me an opportunity to communicate with people—especially young people—that few get the chance to do. Look at what Vince Lombardi accomplished. As far as spiritual influence goes, he had as great an impact on the people he was involved with as the priest down the block."

That, then, is Rote's ultimate goal.

"My dad," he says, "used to tell me that the most important thing in life was to find something to do that would make you happy. 'Be an athlete, a musician, a teacher, whatever,' he would say, 'but be happy.'"

Kyle Rote, Jr., pro soccer player and three-time Superstars winner, appears well on his way to accomplishing that hard-to-achieve goal as well.

MADELINE JACKSON

Olympic Champion (800-meter run)

BEADS OF SWEAT formed across her forehead as she completed her prerace warmup and acknowledged the meet official's call for all finalists in the women's 800-meter run. It was Eugene, Oregon, site of the 1976 United States Olympic Trials, and 28-year-old gospel singer Madeline Manning Jackson was preparing to face yet another moment of truth. A two-time Olympian who had retired from competition following the 1972 Munich Games, she was making a comeback, attempting to join that elite group of American athletes who have competed in three consecutive Olympic Games.

As a twenty-year-old Tennessee State freshman she had captured the gold medal in her specialty at the 1968 Olympic Games in Mexico City, but had failed to place in the 800 four years later in Munich. At twenty-four, she had retired from competition, trading the rigors of daily training and weekend travel to meets for the pursuit of a career and family. But as time passed the urge to run had returned. The competitive spark had not gone out. She came to realize there were still goals to pursue. Also, she had missed the freedom of expression that running had afforded her; the satisfaction of training, of competing, of winning and setting new records. She came back.

And now, as the Olympic Trials were unfolding, she had her goals set not only on earning another trip to the Olympics but had publicly admitted that she felt she was physically and mentally ready to become the first American woman ever to dip below two minutes in the 800 meters. Her U.S. record of 2:00.3 had been set in a dual meet against the Russians in Kiev the previous summer.

As the runners assembled on the track they all walked toward Ms. Jackson, the favorite, the record holder, the seasoned veteran, before taking their appointed places at the starting line. They grouped in a small huddle, eight women who in a matter of minutes would be locked in competitive warfare, and, led by Madeline, prayed. It had been Ms. Jackson's idea. "It was not a prayer for victory or for records," she would later explain. "We simply prayed that each runner would do her best. By doing so we all became winners. The prayer seemed to relax everyone at a time when it is essential that you be relaxed."

Much of Ms. Jackson's competitive strength is directly traceable to her strong Christian faith. One of the primary reasons for her return to competitive athletics, in fact, had been her belief that she could better spread the Word of God and share her faith as an athlete, traveling throughout the world. She had adopted a new motto upon her return to the track and field scene: "Running for Jesus."

And how she ran that June afternoon in Eugene! Her nine-foot stride was devastating, smooth, a picture of effortless power. If there had been concern over her ability to return to the highest level of competition it disappeared quickly as she moved to the front of the pack and seemed to gain strength and confidence with each stride. She won going away with a time of 1:58.81, a new American record. Two more goals had been accomplishd. She had stepped to a higher rung in her chosen field as the first sub-two-minute half-miler in the history of women's track and field in America, and she was once again an Olympian. Then, before the U.S. delegation would leave for Montreal she was dealt yet another honor. Madeline Manning Jackson was selected as the captain of the U.S. women's team.

They were not accomplishments which came without long, tedious hours of hard work, sacrifice, and moments of agony, however.

The Cedar Avenue housing projects sit squarely in the heart of Cleveland's ghetto, a place Madeline Jackson recalls as one where "you either got tough or you got yourself beat up all the time." A gathering place for Cleveland's out-of-work and low income black population, it was hardly the ideal place for a young girl to grow into womanhood. It was an environment marked by despair, frustration, and the gnawing frustration felt by a collection of people down and, in too many cases, on the way out.

By the time she was six years old, Madeline had endured the turmoil of seeing her parents divorce. Her mother, a Christian woman of impressive strength, supported the family by doing housecleaning. Her father was an alcoholic. To stay away from the constant feuding which preceded the breakup, young Madeline spent much of her time in the streets and on nearby playgrounds, playing baseball, football, basketball, and running races. "I was," she is quick to admit today, "the classic example of a tomboy. But I believe strongly that athletes are born. I played with the boys because none of the girls I knew in the project were interested in sports. They weren't competitive. I was, so I went looking for others who were."

By the time Madeline was nine, her mother had remarried to a man who worked as an automobile assemblyman during the week and as a minister on Sundays. He quickly recruited his new stepdaughter to work with the church youth choir. Soon he had her interested in piano lessons. Her world began to broaden, her enthusiasm divided between church activities and the unsupervised playground athletic competition.

"For a long time," she recalls, "my mother worried about me being such a tomboy. She just didn't understand what motivated me. It was just a situation where she wasn't able to see why a little girl would prefer to play a game of baseball with boys and run races instead of playing dolls and acting silly with the other girls. I know she prayed about it a great deal. But she never discouraged me. She let me know she was there to help whenever I needed her, but she was a person who strongly felt it was necessary to allow others to find their own way in life."

Madeline would be a sophomore in high school before ever venturing into the world of organized competition. Her physical education instructor, taking notice of her times in gym class races, suggested to the school's track coach that a visit to the promising youngster might prove profitable to his team. Madeline needed only the slightest encouragement. Soon she was a member of the school girls team and shortly thereafter, running in the Cleveland city meet, won the 220-yard dash, the 440-yard dash and ran on two winning relay teams. A whole new world opened to her—a world which would draw attention to her.

Sandor (Alex) Ferenczy, a native Hungarian who had come to live with relatives in Cleveland twenty years earlier, was the highly successful coach of the Cleveland Track Club, a collection of girls and boys, men and women of all ages and abilities. Among those in attendance at the City Meet the afternoon Madeline captured four blue ribbons, he immediately approached her with the suggestion that she join his team during the summer months to compete in various meets held in the Cleveland area.

Young Madeline was hesitant—not because she was uncertain about expanding her competitive horizons but because she was simply unable to understand Ferenczy's still-thick Hungarian accent. "And my mother had always told me," she says, "never to talk to men I didn't know. So I was a little hesitant to hear him out. Then, too, I really couldn't understand much of what he had to say anyway. So I told him he would just have to talk to my mother about it."

Ferenczy wasted little time meeting Mrs. Manning. She was immediately taken by his friendliness and his enthusiasm—and by the bright future as an athlete he painted for her daughter. In short order the budding young track star in the Manning household was a member-in-good-standing of his Cleveland Track Club. Rated as one of the top women's track and field coaches in the nation, Ferenczy (who has to date coached five Olympians and in 1976 was picked to coach the U.S. women's Olympic squad) quickly recognized the fact that the long-legged schoolgirl with little experience and no real knowledge of running technique was something special. "She thought of herself as a sprinter," he remembers, "but with those long legs it was obvious she would be better suited for the longer distances." Ferenczy suggested the mile. Madeline balked. They compromised on the half-mile, the event the coach had already decided best suited her abilities. "I had to play a little game with her," he grins, "suggesting the mile so the idea of a half-mile would not scare her."

As a high school senior in 1966, Madeline was entered by Ferenczy in her first 880 at the Toronto Maple Leaf Indoor Games against many of the top women half-milers from the United States and Canada. "At the time," her coach remembers, "she was still convinced that she was a sprinter, a 440 runner, but she had been doing some training for the half-mile so it seemed to me time for her to have a try at the distance. Still, she had never run the event competitively and had no idea of how to pace herself. I told her before the race simply to try to stay with the leaders through the first part of the race and then on the final lap see if she could pull away. I really had no idea how she would do, but I felt the exposure to top-flight competition would prove to be a valuable experience as she matured as a half-miler."

Madeline's maturing process took just over two minutes. Not only did she pull away to win the race on the final lap but her winning time was three-tenths of a second better than the existing world indoor 880 record for women. Suddenly everyone was taking notice of the tall, soft-spoken Cleveland teenager. Among those impressed with her abilities was the track coach at Tennessee State University, the long recognized mecca of women's collegiate track, alma mater of such famed Olympic champions as Wilma Rudolph and Wyoma Tyus. Madeline was offered a scholarship and had hardly established herself on the campus before taking yet another giant step in her athletic career. As a freshman she earned a spot on the Mexico City-bound U.S. Olympic team.

In the gaily colored Estadio Olimpico she became one of the biggest surprises of the '68 Games, winning the 800-meter gold medal with a world record clocking of 2:00.9, fifteen yards ahead of Rumania's favored Ilona Silai's 2:02.5. Back home in Cleveland the girl from the Cedar Avenue projects was afforded a heroine's welcome. On the campus of Tennessee State she reigned as one of the school's most celebrated students. Clearly the athletic world now offered Madeline Manning even greater honors to pursue.

But to the surprise of track enthusiasts the world over she would soon announce her retirement from track and her plans to marry Tennessee State football player John Jackson.

Almost from its beginning, however, trouble would plague the relationship. Jackson, himself an outstanding athlete with hopes of a professional football career, suffered a serious back injury during a practice session and was informed by doctors that his athletic career was ended. The frustration of the untimely end to his dream, coupled with the adulation the sports world continued to direct toward his wife, caused him to withdraw, to grow bitter. The marriage began to fall apart and would shortly end in divorce. But not before Madeline had given birth to a son, John, Jr.

"It seemed for a while," she remembers, "that my life had made a complete turnover. There I had been doing well in athletics, winning a gold medal at the Olympics, then getting married and having a child. Suddenly it was all gone, the marriage, my athletic career. It was just me and little John. I didn't know what to do with myself for a while. I prayed that the Lord would give me some direction, give me some idea of what to do with my life."

One of her first major decisions was to return to running. Between time spent in the classroom, at a part-time job, and tending her son, she found time to condition herself for a second try at making the Olympic team. She easily won the U.S. trials but found the going rough at Munich as she was eliminated in the semifinals, placing fifth at 2:02.4. The '72 Games were not a total disappointment, however, as she contributed a strong second leg on the U.S. 1,600-meter relay team which was second to East Germany.

Returning home, she again contemplated her future and recognizing the need to begin a career to support herself and her son, she once again opted to retire from competition. This time her retirement would last two years.

It was early in 1974 when, having returned to Cleveland, Madeline sought out her old club coach Ferenczy.

"I'm going to run again," she told him, "but this time I'm going to do it as a ministry. It will give me an opportunity to spread the Word of God."

Ferenczy, one of those most disappointed when his pupil had decided to retire at what he considered the peak of her career, was delighted. "I'll help you in any way I can," he told her.

Reflecting on that evening when Madeline had returned to the fold, Ferenczy says, "There had been a lot of people who had tried to convince her to return to competition—myself, other coaches, friends, athletes, her family—but it was something she had to work out with the Lord. From that day I saw in her a new purpose. I don't mean that prayer and religious conviction makes Madeline a great runner. That isn't realistic. But those Christian resources give her something extra. I believe that."

After telling Ferenczy she planned to return to training, Madeline remembers a peaceful feeling swept over her. The feeling assured her it was, in fact, the Lord's will for her to return to competitive athletics.

Thus in October of 1974 Madeline Manning Jackson began the long grind that would lead to her third trip to the Olympic Games. By the summer of 1975 she was running better than ever, setting a new American record of 2:00.5 at the women's National Amateur Athletic Union meet, and breaking it just a few weeks later in the Russian duel in Kiev. When she was not running, she was speaking to church gatherings and at meetings of the Fellowship of Christian Athletes.

Yet even as she continued to compete, to lower records and spread her message of faith, things were not always easy. She was teaching gymnastics at the Salvation Army Center in Cleveland, a job whose pay made pinching pennies a constant necessity. To economize she and five-year-old John lived in a one-bedroom, third-floor apartment. They lived comfortably but with few frills.

Economics, in fact, prevented Madeline's possibly adding yet another prestigious gold medal to her collection. Named to the U.S. team which was to compete in the Pan American Games in Mexico City, she was forced to withdraw when team officials asked that all athletes spend four weeks in Mexico City prior to the competition to train in the higher Mexican altitude. "I wanted very much to participate in the Pan Am Games," Ms. Jackson notes, "but to have been away that long would have been impossible. I would have come home to a lot of unpaid bills. It was just one of those things."

There is evidence that some of her financial woes may come to an end in the near future as she embarks on a new career as a gospel singer. Before leaving for Montreal she completed recording an album of religious songs titled "Running for Jesus." There are those who feel confident that her clear soprano voice, developed by years of singing in church choirs, will vault her to new fame.

For Ms. Jackson the singing represents a twofold chance: more financial security for her and her son, and yet another avenue by which she can spread the gospel.

"I hope she is successful at her singing career," said Ferenczy as he sat at the Montreal Olympic Village training table. "She deserves it. During her competitive years she has had to sacrifice a great deal to compete at the level she has attained—entertainment, time for herself, time for her son. But she knows why she is doing it. She has a purpose in life that should be the envy of us all. Because of her faith, her determination, and her willingness to sacrifice, she can come to the end

of a race and reach inside herself and find spiritual resources to push just a little more. That's what champions
are made of."

Things did not go well for Madeline at Montreal.
After running well in her preliminary heat she was never
in contention in the semifinals and failed again to win
a berth in the 800-meter finals. There would be no chance
for a gold medal to go alongside the one she had won
eight years earlier in Mexico City. She felt disappointment and shed a few tears. The hard work, the continued
sacrifice, the hope and expectations had been snuffed out
as women runners from various points on the globe made
her aware that they had now passed her by. The sub-
two-minute half-mile was now big news only in the United
States. In Europe, they are now talking of 1:50. As the
twenty-first Olympiad closed, Ms. Manning knew that her
career as an international competitor was over. This
time she would retire for good.

But not before having blazed a trail for women middle
distance runners in the U.S. Madeline Manning Jackson
competed in three Olympics, she won a gold medal, and
she was the first American to run the half-mile in less
than two minutes.

"God has blessed me," she says. "One gold medal is
enough. Now there are other things for me to do."

No doubt she will do them well.

JOHN HAVLICEK

All-Pro, Boston Celtics

THE TENSION, the nerve-racking anticipation filtering
through the steamy locker room was suffocating, tem-
pered only by occasional nervous conversation or the
high-pitched squeak of sneakers against the moist con-
crete floor. The Boston Celtics were but minutes away

from a game which not only promised great financial reward but would stand as proof positive that their return from the ashes was fully accomplished.

The Celtics, once a professional sports dynasty the likes of which Green Bay, Wisconsin, had never seen, had won eleven National Basketball Association championships in a thirteen-year span in the '50s and '60s. Then, suddenly the Bill Russells and Bob Cousys were gone, retired. Boston sank from the limelight like a rock, to be replaced by teams with nicknames like Lakers, Knicks, and Bucks. The Celtics quickly became little more than just another face in the evergrowing professional basketball crowd.

But now it was May of 1974 and throughout the winter season new hope had echoed through the historic old Boston Garden. Patience, productive drafting, and a few well-timed trades had transformed the Celtics back into contenders. There were even Celtics die-hards who spoke of the oncoming possibility of Dynasty II.

So it had come down to the final game of the best-of-seven NBA playoff series against the Milwaukee Bucks. Each team had won three. The winner of the decisive seventh game would reign as World Champions.

Talking in a quiet, controlled voice in marked contrast to that of his predecessor, Red Auerbach, Celtics coach Tom Heinsohn stood at the blackboard diagramming strategy he had planned for the night's crucial encounter.

Throughout the series the Celtics' scoring had been led by veteran John Joseph Havlicek, a 34-year-old holdover from the previous Dynasty Days, a 6'-5" forward-team captain whose unflagging stamina and competitive desire had prompted many to refer to him as the best all-round player in the game.

"What I want you to do, John," Heinsohn said, "is to

play decoy, draw the defense to you and away from the basket. We've got plenty of people who can score if they get the room."

No one in the room was more enthusiastic about the idea than Havlicek. After 14 years, something like 21,000 points and 35,000 minutes of full speed ahead basketball, individual heroics were relative only when they were coupled with victory.

"Sounds good to me," the Celtics captain said.

The plan worked like a charm through the first half. While Milwaukee defenders were determinedly blocking Havlicek's path to the basket, Jo Jo White, Don Chaney, Paul Silas, and Dave Cowens were scoring at a pace which would provide Boston with a 13-point halftime lead.

Milwaukee, however, made some adjustments of its own at halftime and came back with a rush in the third period, narrowing the Celtics' margin to five points. Havlicek takes up the story from there:

"When they cut the margin to five I began wondering if maybe it was time for me to start shooting some," he says, "but we stuck to our game plan. I made a few points in the second half but mainly continued to play my role as a decoy. Then, near the end of the game, Milwaukee, desperate to close the gap with time running out, turned its attention away from me and gave me a wide open opportunity.

"Driving up the middle of the court, I scored a basket and got a foul shot to boot. It was a big three-point play which put the game out of reach. Minutes later the championship was ours."

For the night, the Celtics' "decoy" managed sixteen points and was then voted the Most Valuable Player of the series. Which is to say it was a fairly typical excerpt from the athletic life of John Havlicek.

Bridgeport, Ohio, sits quietly in the bend of the Ohio River, less than a mile from Wheeling, West Virginia. In the mid-'50s, it claimed a population of 4,300 and a school whose entire twelve-grade enrollment was 560. For the youngsters of the community diversion was simple: church, hunting, fishing, and participating in sports.

It was here, rooted in the serenity of a rural life style, that John Havlicek's athletic career began and came to bloom. He was an All-State quarterback for the football team, led the baseball team in hitting, and was the top scorer for the basketball team. Coffee shop conversation, which always seemed to deal with the glories of Bridgeport High athletics, almost always began and ended with the name Havlicek. If not, the kid who lived across the street from him, Phil Niekro, the school's top pitcher, drew the attention. Later a mainstay pitcher for the Atlanta Braves, Niekro played end on the football team, the primary target for his friend's passes. In basketball he started at one forward spot, John the other.

Even the most versed sports triviast would be hard-pressed to look back to one block in one small community which possessed such athletic talent.

"Looking back," says Niekro, "I honestly think John could have made it professionally in any sport he tried. He was a really fine quarterback. I think he had something like thirty-five scholarship offers. Frankly, when we were growing up I thought that football would be his best sport.

"Woody Hayes at Ohio State wanted him to play football in the worst way, but John told him he was coming to Ohio State only to play basketball."

At Columbus he became a member of one of the most talent-blessed collegiate basketball teams in history. Havlicek, in fact, would play his college ball without star billing, that position being occupied by high-scoring All-American Jerry Lucas.

"I learned about defense when I got to Ohio State," he says. "We had five guys on the team who averaged over 30 points a game in high school and coach (Fred) Taylor needed a defensive forward. That guy was me.

"I became the guy who grinds it out, the kind of player who doesn't receive much publicity because he doesn't shoot or score much."

It was a role the Bridgeport youngster accepted willingly and with enthusiasm. And as he honed his defensive skills he found himself learning more about the offensive phase of the game. To wit:

"I became aware that movement is the most important thing about successfully playing offensive basketball. If you keep moving, the defensive man is going to have to work that much harder. Keep moving constantly and eventually something is going to happen. You run to create a possible scoring situation and to lend confusion to the defense. That, I guess, is the most important lesson I learned from college ball."

By the time the Buckeyes had won the 1960 NCAA championship the entire starting lineup—Lucas, Havlicek, Larry Siegfried, Mel Norwell, and Joe Roberts— was destined for the professional ranks.

It was Norwell, the Buckeye guard who experienced considerable difficulty in pronouncing Havlicek's name, who dealt him the nickname "Hondo" after a then popular John Wayne movie character. The nickname has followed him through his entire pro career.

Despite his modest scoring average Havlicek's talents did not go unnoticed by the professional scouts. Not only did the Celtics make him their first round draft selection but the Cleveland Browns of the National

Football League saw in John the potential to become a wide receiver. They selected him in the seventh round of their draft.

"I had," Havlicek says, "enjoyed football in high school and the idea of playing again intrigued me. And I felt like I had a pretty good chance to make it. I had good hands, had run the 40 in 4.6, and had the size. I felt pretty confident about my chances when I reported to camp."

That confidence was justified through most of the demanding pre-season training. It eventually boiled down to a choice between the impressive converted basketball player and Gary Collins as the Browns were forced to cut a player to reach the 40-man roster limit set by the NFL. Collins stayed and John, admittedly crushed, went off to the Celtics' camp.

He was aware there were those who had openly questioned Auerbach's having picked him as the team's first draft selection. Sure, the kid could play, they admitted. He could rebound and played excellent defense. But scoring was the name of the professional game. Could he score?

Auerbach, now president and general manager of the Celtics, admits that he was operating on instinct to some degree when he picked Havlicek. "Actually," he says, "I only saw him play twice as a collegian and both times he had rather poor games. Still, there was something about him. He was quick and boy, could he run. He moved like liquid energy, with no visible working parts. He was a 100 percent kind of ball player and I felt he could help us."

Score an understatement for Mr. Auerbach.

With such sharpshooters as Russell, K.C. and Sam Jones, Cousy, Heinsohn, and Frank Ramsey, the Celtics were hardly in dire need of additional offensive firepower. Thus rookie Havlicek found himself spending his playing time in the familiar role of a defensive specialist.

In time, however, Havlicek would move into the famed Celtics sixth man spot vacated by retired Sam Jones. But before the transition could be successfully completed, Auerbach had to call John into his office. "You've got to start shooting the ball," he said. "Everyone in the league sags off of you when you've got the ball because they know you aren't going to put it up. Show them differently."

Havlick recalls the discussion as if it were yesterday. "He only had to tell me once," John says. "I knew I could shoot. I just hadn't felt it was my role up to that point. Thereafter, I began scoring."

And scoring. Past the 20,000 mark in the 1973–74 season, becoming only the eighth player in NBA history to achieve that plateau.

Thus over a span of sixteen years Havlicek's role with the Celtics had drastically changed; from a sparingly used rookie whose on-court presence seldom gained the attention of the press to a full-fledged superstar, All-Pro, scoring leader, bell cow of the revamped Celtics. He is now the man the rest of the team looks to for leadership, the individual called upon to take the crucial shot.

"When I came here," he says, "I was the young kid who spoke only when spoken to. Now I'm the senior citizen, the guy the other players look to for answers. It's a nice feeling."

He is not one to lead by words when actions will suffice, however. "Athletes," he points out, "respect ability and naturally the people who have been around the longest get the most respect. It boils down to a matter of your character and style of play and your ability to perform when it is difficult.

"I like to think I've matured a great deal during my career. Personal accomplishments no longer are the big thing for me. I enjoy the feeling of being a part of something successful and playing a part in that success. When I was in college my coach told us that there were many poor teams who had one or two great players. Good teams have five who work well together. It is amazing what can be accomplished when no one cares who gets the credit."

Such a philosophy as this has earned Havlicek the valued role of leadership in Boston.

There are those who will tell you there is something mystical, uncanny about the manner in which the Celtics' superstar is able to perform. "I'm convinced," said one sportswriter, "that the original idea for the TV show 'The Six Million Dollar Man' came from someone who has seen John Havlicek play basketball."

Rod Hundley, former Lakes performer and now a color commentator for CBS pro basketball telecasts, puts it this way: "He's had a few pulled muscles along the way but nothing really serious. Any other player who tried to run as much as John does would have died of old age ten years ago."

"He's a freak," says another former Laker, Jerry West. "His endurance is incredible." Adds LA's Pat Riley, "There's not a man in the league who can stay up with him for a whole game and survive. His body is made to go on forever."

A couple of seasons ago Havlicek was sidelined with a slight leg muscle pull but in short order he was back in the lineup. It was a return that was of great relief to backup man Silas who was laboring in the role of

Boston's sixth man until called upon to replace Havlicek.

"When John's healthy," he explained, "I go back into my sub role which is great with me because I want to play another five or six years. There's no way in the world I could ever make it trying to fill in for John and trying to go at his pace. He's the only player in the league who can go full speed for forty-eight minutes."

Or more if necessary. Enroute to the championship in '74 the fast-break Celtics and methodical Bucks waged battle through a double overtime before Milwaukee finally won. Havlicek played the entire fifty-eight minutes.

"I was so keyed up," he would later note, "that I honestly believe I could have played another overtime. But, yes, it was hard. I had people tell me after the game was over that I didn't even look like myself. Afterward, I couldn't eat or sleep or anything."

Less than forty-eight hours later, however, he was back on court to play his vital decoy role in that championship game.

To Havlicek the explanation is simple. "You have to lick your mind," he says. "If you tell yourself you're tired, you are going to be. You've got to tell yourself you aren't tired and keep pushing yourself. I'm ready to go all the time. It's just something God has blessed me with.

"Consciously the only thing I try to do is eat well and get my sleep. But mentally you have to have pride and motivation to accomplish the goals you set for yourself. When you reach a certain level of efficiency you have to try to maintain it over a long haul."

It should also be noted that Havlicek possesses what the medical experts term a superbly efficient cardiovascular system. His heart has been measured at an amazing

46 beats per minute—something like 30 beats slower than that of most fit men in their 30s.

Despite all the superlatives, the continuing flow of honors and awards, time is now running out on John Havlicek, basketball player. Night after night of 48-minute basketball, the physical punishment and the grind of coast-to-coast travel have taken their toll. At 36, an age when most men are coming into their most productive years in their chosen careers, Havlicek is considered an old man. It is a fact of which he is well aware.

"I know," he says, "that retirement is only a few years away. Right now I feel like I can play forever, but I know the day will come to hang them up." (He did announce his retirement at the end of the 1977 season.)

"I'll play as long as I enjoy it and am able to contribute," he once said. "For me the game has always been fun. Oh, I dislike training camps and consider road trips nothing better than a necessary evil. And I've got a permanently sore right wrist, the result, I'm sure, of a couple of hundred thousand one-handed set shots. But, each year once I get into shape I find it just as much fun as when I first started playing."

But, yes, he admits he's giving more time of late to thought of his future. "For years I've been working in the off-season as a manufacturer's representative in Worthington, Ohio. I expect to join the firm full-time when I retire."

He admits it will be no easy transition. He will miss the competition, the camaraderie and, yes, the spotlight which is forever focused on professional athletes.

"My confidence for that transition," he says, "is bolstered by a habit I began as a teenager. Each day I read a devotional with a Bible verse and prayer. From that practice, from my association with many fine people, from the influence of wonderful parents and the support of my great wife, I have developed a faith and an attitude about life.

"It's simply that each of us has a role to play, and whatever it is we should do it with our whole body, mind, and soul."

It is an attitude, a faith, John Havlicek has carried with him for a lifetime.

MEL KENYON

Three-time Midget Race Car Champion

THE OLD LANGHORNE Speedway is gone now, a
grudging victim of what city fathers are wont to call
progress. The land where it once stood simply became
more valuable to real estate developers than it was to
those who used to come faithfully to watch many of the

world's greatest drivers grind around its treacherous turns and negotiate its too narrow, too short straightaways.

For the first forty years of its existence Langhorne was a dirt track whose surface was, depending on the time of the year, bumpy, hard, loose, or, on occasion when a late evening Pennsylvania thunderstorm passed over, a quagmire. It was always a dangerous track. Drivers dreaded racing on it, yet they always came— for the handsome purses promised the winners, for the prestige a victory at Langhorne afforded, and for the challenge the track itself offered. There, probably more definitely than on any racing stop in America, a driver faced an added adversary. He would not only match his abilities against other drivers but against the track as well. Thus Langhorne was legendary in auto racing circles.

Even after it was paved and the banks on the turns improved in 1965 it was a course to be traveled with the utmost caution. Get past Langhorne, drivers on the United States Auto Club (USAC) championship trail used to say, and your chances of finishing the season in one piece improved dramatically.

It was a fact of which Mel Kenyon, the man most racing experts regard as the best midget car driver in the country, was well aware when he entered a championship car event there in 1965. As was the habit of the Lebanon, Indiana, native, Kenyon had carefully studied the track. He knew its high risk areas, the soft spots in the newly laid blacktop surface, the proper grooves to take coming out of the turns. And he was confident he could navigate the problem areas.

But on this particular day the fault would neither rest with the condition of the track nor his own time-proven driving ability. It would be Kenyon's car which would fail, bringing its driver closer to death than most survive to look back upon.

The race was still young and the field still tightly grouped when his engine threw a rod. Having trouble controlling the car, the veteran Kenyon brushed the track retaining wall slightly and then began sliding to a halt when two other cars roared into the straightaway and crashed into him. The impact split his fuel tank open and suddenly his car was engulfed in a wall of flame. The collision had snapped Kenyon's head back against the roll bar behind him, knocking him unconscious. To further complicate the situation, the speedway fire truck was parked almost a mile from the burning wreckage.

Fellow drivers Joe Leonard and Jim Hurtubise, seeing the orange flames which covered Kenyon's car, quickly pulled their cars off the track and raced to his aid, one unlocking the shoulder strap while the other worked to loosen the unconscious driver's seat belt. Forced to retreat several times by the intense heat, they were finally able to drag Kenyon from the inferno.

But not before he had suffered third-degree burns over 40 percent of his body. Both legs, his left shoulder, left arm, neck, and face were badly burned. He was immediately flown to Brooke Army Medical Center in San Antonio, a hospital famed for its handling of the most severe burn cases.

A team of twelve doctors evaluated the condition of the then thirty-two-year-old driver and told him he could expect to be hospitalized for at least nine months. For the first month Kenyon's wife Marieanne, constantly at his bedside, fed him, bathed him, and whispered constant prayers that her husband of just a year would pull through the painful ordeal.

The pain would become so unbearable that Kenyon would yell himself hoarse (as a result he still has a voice problem today). Then, when he could no longer yell, he bit into a roll of gauze until all of his teeth had worked loose.

Complicating his despair was the fact that doctors had begun removing the dead skin from his left hand. It quickly became apparent that most of the hand would have to be removed. For Mel Kenyon, professional auto driver, that was the greatest pain of all. How, he repeatedly asked, would he ever drive again with only a stub for a left hand?

The agony seemed to stretch endlessly, a nightmare from which he could not awake. Once the skin grafting procedure began he could no longer lie in bed and was thus forced to sit and lean over a table top to sleep. The initial pain was at last decreasing but the complications continued to mount. The skin grafts were not healing satisfactorily. Kenyon, near the breaking point, tottering on an emotional edge he had never before experienced, suddenly became aware that he needed help beyond that his own courage and the doctors' talents could supply.

·"I had listened to Marieanne cry and pray for weeks," he remembers. "I cried and prayed with her, but I lacked the faith to go along with my prayers. She saw that I was just about at the end of my rope and began explaining how knowing Christ might well be the only thing that could make the difference in my life.

"I knew I needed help and the more I listened to her, the more convinced I became that only Jesus Christ could help me. So I asked him to come into my life."

Today Kenyon is quick to point out that he was not healed overnight. The pain did not immediately disappear nor did the anxieties of what the future held subside. But positive changes did begin to happen—but slowly at first. His wounds began to heal and his strength began coming back to him. And with the healing and strength came renewed motivation.

In four months Mel Kenyon walked out of the hospital, a full five months ahead of the target date the doctors had given him. And even before he had taken leave of his hospital bed he had made up his mind about a decision he had spent many sleepless nights considering. Hand or no hand, he was going to race again.

But it would not be easy.

Kenyon's father, Everett, and brother, Don, both veterans of auto racing and top-notch mechanics, set to work to design a custom glove with a metal socket for him. Once the glove was laced onto his hand, Kenyon would attach it to a metal pin located on the steering wheel.

"After I was able to convince officials I could properly handle a car," Kenyon says, "I was given a permit to drive midget cars again with the idea being that I could be elevated (to driving stocks and championship model cars) at the end of the year if I proved I was capable."

Just nine months after the Langhorne accident, Mel Kenyon broke the world record for half-mile dirt tracks in a race in Phoenix. So impressive were his performances in that 1966 season, in fact, that championship car owner Fred Gerhardt offered him a job driving one of his entries in the Indianapolis 500. Kenyon finished a highly respectable fifth in his rookie year at the fabled old brickyard. Even the most die-hard doubters were finally convinced that he was back, better than ever, with a bright racing future still ahead of him.

At forty-three he could look back on eight Indy 500 appearances—once placing as high as third in the rain-shortened 1973 event, earning fourth place money another time—as well as impressive records in a variety of major championship races. Yet he remains, by choice, a midget car racer first and foremost. Three times he has been crowned as the USAC midget champion and is fast approaching the eighth feature race victory of his twenty-one-year career.

He talks of retirement occasionally now, but close followers of the vagabond midget racing circuit pay him little mind. "No one quits while they're still driving as well as Mel does," says brother Don, "and believe me, Mel hasn't lost an inch."

If anything, he has become more dedicated to his chosen sport. "It's the only type of motorsports left that is any fun," he says. "Indy car races are all business; no fun anymore. Road racing is getting to be the same way.

"But I still get a big kick out of the midgets. I enjoy the circuit, the people, the competition, and the fans who come out. It's a special kind of life."

Indeed it is. There are those who will insist that for one to succeed as a midget car driver he would do well to have, in addition to driving skills and a bonus of stamina, a bit of gypsy blood flowing through his veins.

A typical summer for Kenyon and his family goes something like this: Loaded into their camper, pulling the race car behind, they make a sweep through the Rocky Mountain area, racing almost nightly in a Colorado-Utah-Idaho circuit. Then there is just time for a quick two-day dash back to the Midwest for weekend races in Hinsdale and Springfield, Illinois, and Schererville, Indiana. Then back to the mountains.

The Kenyons thrive on it. "It's not all that rugged,"

Mel says, wrapping a cushion of gauze around the nub of his left hand before fitting on his glove prior to yet another feature race. "In fact, it's more enjoyable now than it was some years ago. These new campers have most of the comforts of home and you can really enjoy the travel, take your family along, and not be out too much money."

Money, despite the time-worn legends of big-time auto racing, is not Kenyon's primary motivation. If it were, he no doubt would have long ago dismissed the midget car circuit and given more serious concentration to the championship cars. The top half dozen midget racers active today seldom gross more than $20,000 to $25,000 a season.

"What you have to do," Mel says, "is budget your money. Keep the priorities in mind. Naturally, you've got to keep your equipment running in top condition. Fortunately, for a midget's car that's not too hard to do unless you get completely wiped out in a crash. A new car, complete and ready to run, will cost something in the neighborhood of $13,800. That figure won't buy the parts for an Indy car these days."

Kenyon is able to cut additional corners by growing much of the food he and his family eat while on the circuit. He and his brother own a four-acre plot near their Indiana home and have turned it into a huge vegetable garden. Both wives do a lot of canning and stock the camper with quart jars filled with blackeyed peas, green beans, squash, and so on. They seldom eat in restaurants, opting for mobile home cooking, and almost always sleep in the camper rather than paying a motel bill.

It is, in many respects, a spartan kind of life style.

The seasons, though shorter now than they used to be, still call for as many as fifty events. Stamina is a basic necessity.

"I honestly feel," Kenyon says, "that driving midgets calls for more skill than driving an Indy car. In midget racing, the driver makes much more difference.

"The tracks we run on are obviously smaller; often only a quarter mile and probably not even quite that long in some cases. They have very short straightaways, so you're constantly turning, always working.

"And the tracks differ so much you're always changing suspension setups. More times than not, you don't have much practice time so you wind up guessing and just hoping that you've hit on the proper setup.

"You're always on the move from one city to the next—a lot like rodeo performers, I guess—so there's little time to work on your car. It has its frustrations, believe me.

"Still, there's that feeling of accomplishment you get after performing well that just can't be duplicated anywhere else. I've had a rewarding career. I got a second chance, something not too many people get, the day I walked out of that hospital.

"I thank God for that every day of my life."

EARL CAMPBELL

University of Texas Halfback
1977 Heisman Trophy Winner

THE DRESSING ROOM of the historic old Cotton
Bowl stadium was awash with jubilation as players
shook each other's hands, erupted in rattling victory
yells, and accepted the congratulations from fans who

were managing to elbow their way into the celebration. The University of Texas, a decided underdog just hours earlier, had put together an amazing display of football for sixty grueling minutes and had defeated arch rival Oklahoma, 13-6.

It was a significant achievement for numerous reasons. The powerful Sooners had been picked by many to reign as the 1977 national champions and had come into the game on the heels of a highly publicized victory over Ohio State. It had been seven long, trying years since the Longhorns had been able to leave Dallas, the annual site of this fabled border rivalry, with a victory over the Big Eight powerhouse. Texas had scored three lopsided victories prior to the game but the caliber of their competition left many unanswered questions as to how good a team they might really be. The game would provide Fred Akers, the youthful Texas coach who had stepped into the very large shoes of retiring Darrell Royal, with his first opportunity to register a major victory as the Longhorn football boss.

And while such victories are historically fashioned from precision work by an entire team, there was one young man who would stand above the rest when the day was over, praised at game's end by coaches and fans of Texas and Oklahoma alike. A powerful, determined Texas halfback named Earl Christian Campbell, going to battle against the Sooners for the fourth time in his storybook collegiate career, had played the game as if there were no tomorrow. "That," said Akers, hearing the observation through the tumult of the dressing quarters, "is nothing new. That's how Earl Campbell plays every football game he goes into."

It is an attitude which, no doubt, accounted for the fact that he had reported for work on that particular sun-drenched October Saturday as the leading collegiate scorer in the nation. He was the main gear in a high-scoring Texas offensive machine which was leading the nation in total offense and scoring, and was fast closing in on the all-time Southwest Conference individual rushing record. Also, he was, in this his final season of college football, being touted as one of the chief contenders for the Heisman Trophy, the honor dealt annually to the top college football player in the country.

It had been his touchdown which lifted the Longhorns to victory, his grinding, twisting, stubborn 123 yards rushing which had made him the day's leading ground gainer—and hero.

It was, then, an ideal time for the senior All-American pick to take a seat in front of his locker and await the swarm of newsmen who would ask him everything from what he had for breakfast to how it felt the instant he crashed across the goal line for the game-winning score. They would no doubt hang on his every word, his every description of the titanic battle which had just taken place, and sing him high praise in the next morning's editions. It was an ideal situation for a Heisman Trophy candidate. For it has been said—and with proven validity —that publicity almost as much as performance often determines the winner of the prestigious award.

And with all that clearly in mind Earl Campbell showered quickly, dressed, answered a few questions from reporters, and then politely excused himself. "Hey, Earl, where are you going in such a big hurry?" asked a teammate savoring the upset triumph, the perfect 4–0 record the team had achieved, and the attention of the fans and the media.

Earl smiled broadly. "My mom came up for the game," he said. "She's waiting outside for me right now.

I'm going to go visit with her before we have to leave."

So much, then, for campaigning for the Heisman. Earl Campbell, a young man of maturity beyond his years, had decided long ago to let his actions speak for his football abilities. At that particular moment he had something more important to do than campaign for awards.

He had to go see the lady whose strict discipline and stern guidance had enabled him to be where he was in the first place.

"I know," he says, "that everyone thinks his mother is special but, to me, mine is the greatest lady I've ever known. She worked hard to help me make something of myself; to make me see that there were opportunities for someone who worked hard. Someday soon I hope I can start repaying a little bit of what I owe her. This time next year I'd like to have her a new house built and a new car to drive and maybe a little money to take her on some trips now and then."

Clearly Earl Campbell is thinking ahead to the big money professional football is offering athletes with a special talent for running with the football. That is his goal. It is the brass ring he has been chasing since he was scoring touchdowns for Tyler High, leading his team to the Texas state Class AAAA championship, and causing veteran football observers to call him the greatest schoolboy running back in the state's history.

Now a young man of strong convictions and a unique dedication, he refuses to be distracted from the primary goal of his athletic life. Texas' Darrell Royal, who coached Campbell for three years before retiring from coaching at the end of last season, says, "Earl is one of the most serious young men I've ever been around. There is little room for nonsense in his life. He's too busy trying to make something of himself. Oh, I'm not saying he walks around with his brow wrinkled all the time; he loves to laugh. It's just that he's generally not the fella who is making the laughter. A sportswriter will probably have a hard time getting a lot of colorful anecdotes and clever answers from him."

What one gets instead is a philosophy born of simple, sincere Southern Baptist Christianity. "The Lord," he says, "blesses us all with a gift, and he expects us to use it. My gift is the ability to play football, and it is important to me to be the very best at it that I can."

Even so, he admits that at one time he lacked the positive direction so evident in his life style today. Of the eleven children born to B. C. and Ann Campbell, Earl showed signs in early adolescence of becoming his family's problem child. He speaks now of these troubled times without the indulgence which generally accompanies reminiscences of one's youthful escapades. "By the time I was in high school," he says soberly, "I was smoking a pack of cigarettes a day, doing a little hustling with a pool cue, shooting craps, drinking—the whole number. Man, I didn't spend one minute thinking about the future. I just figured one day I'd get out of high school, get me a car, and, you know, just bum around."

Her son's rash behavior was all too obvious to Ann Campbell, a hard-working, strong-willed woman forced to shoulder the entire burden of raising her large family after her husband died when Earl was nine. Without hesitation, she took on her son's discipline. And those who know Ann Campbell are aware that when she sets her mind to something, there is every reason to believe she will succeed.

"She kept after me," Earl remembers, "telling me that I had a chance to make something of myself because of my athletic ability. She said I would always be sorry if I threw that chance away. Then, she would tell me that because I was a good football player there would be a lot of younger kids looking up to me, and they were going to be disappointed in what they saw if I didn't straighten up. The more she talked, the more I began to realize she was making sense.

"And, too, about that time I was really getting into football, seeing that maybe it was something I had a special talent for. My mother challenged me to see how good I could be, how far football could carry me."

Which is where pursuit of the Heisman comes into the Campbell picture.

A superlative senior season, he was aware, could serve as the springboard to the prestige and capital that most gifted college athletes harbor in their dreams. Professional scouts had been aware of the big Tyler running back's abilities since he earned All-Southwest Conference recognition as a freshman. The following year, Earl was again named to the conference squad and to the All-American team selected by the nation's college football coaches. As a fullback for Royal, Campbell spent much of his junior year sidelined by a hamstring injury, but still played enough to rank as the Longhorns' leading rusher. Thus he entered his final year of collegiate eligibility just 531 yards shy of the UT career rushing record of 3,230 yards. Even before the season got underway Campbell, pronounced fit and ready to run by team physicians, was picked to virtually every pre-season All-American team.

And Earl, a youngster who manages successfully to blend confidence and modesty, made no attempt to hide the fact that he would like to add the trophy to his already impressive collection. To be sure, the recognition is dealt annually to only the most rare of football talents. Previous winners were virtually assured some degree of lasting eminence in American sports—Doak Walker, Roger Staubach, O. J. Simpson, and Tony Dorsett, to name a few.

The sixty-pound trophy, standing thirteen and one-half inches high, is an impressive piece of craftsmanship. Its bronze figure of a turn-of-the-century football player mounted on a black onyx base recognizes "the best college football player in the country."

To claim it for his own, however, would not become an obsession for the 6′-1″, 220-pound running back. "Awards," he says, "are just like records. They're nice to get and, yes, they make you feel good, but they're not the reason you play the game. If they come, fine; if not and you can tell yourself that you've done your best, then that's enough."

Bill Morgan, sports information director for the Southwest Conference, asked Campbell what kind of person he would vote for it it were his responsibility to select the Heisman winner. "I'd look for a guy," Earl replied, "who was a great man off the field as well as on it, not just with his teammates but with people who aren't in football, who don't really even care about football. I'd want a guy who knows people, kids especially, are looking at him to judge what kind of man he is. So far as athletic ability goes, I'd look for someone who can do a lot of things well. If he's a runner, I'd want to see how tough he runs. A lot of guys can dodge one or two tacklers, but I'd want to see if he can break tackles when two or three guys hit him."

Akers, talking with Morgan following the interview,

said, "I'm sure Earl did not intend it that way, but what he did was describe himself perfectly."

Heisman awards and All-American honors, however, are not the ultimate aspirations of Earl Campbell, the athlete. Pro football (and the things its money will enable him to accomplish) stands as his goal.

"There is no question in my mind," says Gil Brandt, player personnel director for the Dallas Cowboys, "that Earl has a great future as a professional player." Already, in fact, there are those who compare him to the legendary Jim Brown, former Cleveland Browns' great.

"I've thought about playing pro football since I first really got turned on to the game," Earl admits. "I'd like very much to earn my living playing professionally for a while.

"It's my chance to make some big money," he admits freely, "money that I need to do some of the things I want to do." Like building a house for his mother and purchasing some acreage near Tyler where he hopes one day to open a camp for underprivileged children. "A place," he says, "where they can have fun and rap and learn how to set some worthwhile goals for themselves. That's my big dream, the thing I want most of all. I really dig kids, love to be around them and talk to them. If I can help a few of them, then I can feel I've made some kind of contribution to this world."

As he speaks, another side of Earl Campbell comes into focus—the Earl Campbell one does not see from a 50-yard line vantage point on a Saturday afternoon.

Akers has already become acquainted with both sides of his star player's nature.

"I've never been associated with a young man more sincere than Earl is," he says. "He genuinely cares about people—about you, about me, his family, teammates, other students on the campus. He's always eager to speak to youth groups and is very active in the Fellowship of Christian Athletes.

"I'm talking about a person I honestly believe is the best college football player in America. What I'm also saying is that his football ability is just one of the things that impress me about him. I believe his sincerity and dedication to his religious convictions will bring him his greatest success."

Whatever that success proves to be, Campbell undoubtedly will place much of the credit elsewhere. "The Lord is in control of my life," he says. "Whatever I'm able to do is up to him. All I can do is work and pray and give whatever I do my best effort. After I'm satisfied I've done that, then I know the rest is up to him. He's not going to make it easy. In fact, you show me a successful man—successful by whatever measure you want to choose—and I'll show you a man who has had his share of bumps and bruises and failures along the way. That's the way life works."

Earl Campbell is not delivering a sermon. That's not his way. He is simply stating his viewpoint. "Sure, I'm proud I'm a Christian, proud that The Man is in my life, proud that I pray and read my Bible, but I get concerned sometimes when some writer makes a big deal about it. I'm no different from anyone else. I sin, fall flat on my face now and then. But I try to live by a rule my mother was finally able to teach me: when you fall, get up as quickly as you can. The Man forgives; he says, 'Hey, it's okay, start over; try to do a little better next time.' "

Alvin Cartwright, a Longhorn reserve, offers further insight into the kind of person Campbell is. "I came to

school thinking I was a pretty hotshot football player,"
he says. "But I wasn't getting to play as much as I
thought I should. I was having a lot of problems coping
with that and finally went to Earl to talk about it. I told
him I was fed up, that I didn't think I was getting a fair
chance and that I was going to quit and transfer to
North Texas.

"He sat there and heard me out, and then asked if I
had talked to the coach about it. I told him that I
hadn't and he said if I was going to leave I owed it
to the coach to talk it over with him. Then Earl looked
me right in the eye and said, 'Okay, man, I'm your
friend, I'm on your side, but I'm going to give it to you
straight: you quit here and go to North Texas. What
if you don't make it there, either? You going to quit
there, too? You going to keep running away from the
problem and keep quitting?' That made me stop and
think."

Alvin Cartwright remained a member of the UT
squad. He didn't rise to the stardom he hoped for, but he
had the resolve to stand his ground and try to make
his place.

Campbell, elected as one of the team captains at the
beginning of his senior year, was a sounding board for
many of the Longhorn players. It is yet another proof
of the respect he has earned from his peers.

"When Earl talks," says roommate Alfred Jackson,
"everybody listens. I remember a couple of years ago a
bunch of us were sitting around, just shooting the bull,
and a couple of guys got into an argument. One guy
picks up this chair and starts after the other one. Now
Earl hadn't said much all evening, but when it looked
like something was about to happen, he got up, went
over to the dude with the chair, pinned him up against

the wall, and said in a very soft voice, 'I think you better put that chair down . . . and sit in it.' That's all it took to calm things down."

His dormitory door has always been open—to his younger twin brothers, Tim and Steve, who are also members of the UT team, to frustrated freshmen having difficulty coping with the transition from high school to college, to nonfootball playing friends. "Part of my responsibility," Earl observes, "has been to help young players to improve in whatever way I can. When I first came to Texas I had help from Roosevelt Leaks (now with the Baltimore Colts). He was a senior, an All-American and all that, but he always had time to work with me. I'll never forget it."

In many ways, Earl Campbell is something of a rarity. Back in Tyler at age five, he worked alongside his mother, brothers, and sisters in the rose fields, doing his small boy part to help the family keep together and make ends met. As a fourth grader, he spent Sunday afternoons playing sandlot football with high school boys, holding his own. After his mother's wise counsel, then, came full-blown athletic stardom. Always, along the way was the stern, caring mother who worked at a variety of jobs, usually for low pay, to feed and clothe her children.

One day, perhaps, not far ahead, odds are that she will be moving from the too-small frame house on a farm road across from a Tyler junk yard into a new one built by her son's earnings from professional football. When that times comes it will be nice for Ann Campbell to display in her living room the Heisman Trophy engraved with her son's name.

"That," says Earl, "would make it perfect."

On the night of 8 December 1977, Earl Campbell,

dressed uncomfortably in a tuxedo, became the first player from The University of Texas ever to win the Heisman Trophy. Amid the applause from the fifteen hundred attending the award ceremony in the grand ballroom of the New York Hilton Hotel, the young man selected as the best collegiate football player in the nation slowly made his way to the speaker's stand.

There he accepted the prestigious trophy from Jay Berwanger, first winner of the award forty-three years earlier and then stood silent for a moment. He would eventually speak of the help of his teammates and his coaches and of how he would do his best to represent what the Heisman Trophy stands for. But his first words were directed to Ann Campbell who had been flown to New York courtesy of a Tyler couple for whom she had worked as a maid for twenty years.

"Mom," Earl said, "you remember when I was a kid and would get into trouble and come to you and say, 'Hey, mom, I'm in trouble'? Well, here I am in trouble again. I don't know what to say."

At that particular moment, with the highest award college football has to offer cradled in his arm and his mother sitting in the audience, smiling, savoring her son's achievement, no words were necessary.

Later in 1978, Campbell signed a contract with the Houston Oilers. It was anticipated that he would be their first-round draft choice, and he was.

CINDY Mᶜ INGVALE

Olympic Diver

IF YOU MEET Cynthia Potter McIngvale most any Sunday afternoon you might think she's a mild-mannered suburban Dallas housewife who spends her time loafing around the house and mixing sauce for backyard barbecues with her husband Jim, a twenty-six-year-old ex-football player and current owner of a local physical fitness center.

But that's only what Cindy McIngvale would like us to believe—at least on her day of rest. The truth is that, for the other six days of the week, Cindy is a petite (5'1", 98 pounds) package of perpetual motion and the United States' premiere woman diver. She works out daily for four hours at the Southern Methodist University diving pool to build stamina, smooth slight flaws in form, experiment with new and more difficult dives, and sharpen up for whatever competition is next on her schedule.

At age twenty-six, McIngvale has already assured herself a prominent place in the history of diving. A bronze medalist in the '76 Montreal Olympics, she has been nominated three times for the Sullivan Award ('71, '76 and '77), which is given to the nation's top amateur athlete. She's also been selected for the All-American diving team nine times, and twice been picked World Diver of the Year for the three-meter springboard event.

Just fourteen days after climbing to the winners' stand in Montreal to accept a bronze for her three-meter springboard diving, McIngvale was competing in Decatur, Alabama, for her twenty-third and twenty-fourth national championship titles. "I realized I wasn't tired mentally or physically after the Olympics," she says. "I knew I was in top shape, so I could see no legitimate reason to avoid competing in the nationals."

Those wins plus two more at the 1977 AAU indoor nationals in Austin upped McIngvale's national title total to twenty-six, tying her with the immortal Pat McCormick for the most national wins and putting McIngvale within touching distance of her goal to win more national diving titles than any other woman in the history of the sport.

Since her first national-level competition in 1968 (winning the national one-meter title that year), McIngvale has had few layoffs of any duration—except on Sundays. It is rare, she insists, that the rigors of the sport begin to wear on her. "The truth of the matter is," she says, "I find all aspects of competitive diving enjoyable. I even look forward to my workouts. I'm fortunate in that I have found something that has been—and still is—a lot of fun for me, as well as being very satisfying."

The only time McIngvale seriously contemplated retirement came after the 1972 Olympic Games in Munich. Entering the competition as the top-ranked American female diver and a strong candidate to win a medal, she suffered a serious foot injury during a practice session just two days before the opening ceremonies. What she feared at first to be a broken ankle was later diagnosed as a sprain, but team doctors still urged her to withdraw from the competition. "I had worked too hard to get to that point," she recalls, "and I knew if I was able to walk out to the end of the board I would dive. I thought about it a great deal and said a lot of prayers. Not prayers asking God to let me go out and perform well enough to win a gold medal or anything like that; just to help me compete in the event which I had worked so hard to get to. The Lord has blessed me with a gift, an ability which I am proud of, but I have never asked him to help me to perform beyond my capabilities. I have strong faith and because of that faith I felt I should make every effort to go ahead and participate even though I knew down deep that my chances of performing well weren't very good."

Thus, competing with great pain and the frustrating knowledge that she was unable to give her best effort, she finished a disappointing seventh in the three-meter springboard event.

"That," she says, "was the first time in my life that competing was not really enjoyable. I had never competed with that kind of pain. It took all of the thrill out of the Olympics for me. I was disappointed, not so much because I did not win a medal, but because I had not been able to perform up to the capabilities I knew I had."

When she returned home, the then twenty-one-year-old diver found it necessary to make a close evaluation of her athletic motivations. "In addition to the foot injury," she says, "I had stretched some ligaments in my lower back. After a while the foot began to heal, but the back problem stayed with me. Finally, I went to several doctors, and each advised me to give up thoughts of returning to diving and risking further injury to my back. Though I had not completely made up my mind that I wanted to continue to compete, I knew I wasn't ready to accept the doctors' opinions. So I just kept going to other doctors."

She finally consulted a California specialist who told her what she wanted to hear, and then designed a special brace to help her continue in competition. "At that moment," she says, "I realized it would be necessary to give my back an opportunity to completely heal. So I decided to stay out of competition for a full year, then give it another try."

After her graduation from Indiana University in 1973, Cynthia Potter moved back home to Houston and took a job substitute teaching and performing with the Allegro Ballet Company. "The ballet work enabled me to bring one of my fantasies to life," she remembers. "I had taken dance since I was three years old and there was a time in my life when the thing I wanted most in the world was to be a professional ballet dancer. But, if you'll look, you'll see that there aren't too many well-known dancers who are only 5'1". So being able to perform with even a small professional group was a tremendous thrill for me. And it was a great way to improve the coordination needed in diving."

For ten months she did not so much as step onto a diving board. Diving, however, was constantly in the back of her mind. The layoff, she reflects, gave her time to plan what she hoped to accomplish upon her return to competition. "There were things I wanted to try—more difficult dives—that I hadn't been able to experiment with while I was in college. At Indiana there were so many outstanding swimmers and divers that there was a highly competitive atmosphere even in practice. You were forced to concentrate on your list of competition dives constantly, just to maintain your position on the team. Then, when you're preparing for the Olympics, you find yourself working with the same restrictions. You simply don't have the luxury of time needed to expand your list of dives. Instead, you constantly work to perfect the dives you're going to do."

When it seemed to her that she was ready to get back on the board in 1974, McIngvale moved to Dallas, where she could work under the expert eye of SMU diving coach Bryan Robbins. "He's an outstanding coach," Cindy says, "and he is willing to let his divers make their own decisions about what dives they want to do. Once that is determined, he works with you to help you develop them."

It was a combination of Robbins' encouragement and her own determination that ultimately resulted in Cindy's achieving another of her goals. At the '77 indoor nationals she became the first woman ever to successfully execute a 3½ somersault off the three-meter board. "It was something I felt I was capable of," she admits, "but I wasn't sure I could score that well with it. I went into the competition thinking I would be very satisfied with a 5.0." (It is rare for a diver to get more than 8 of a possible 10 points.) In the preliminaries the judges awarded her a 6.65. She received a 5.55 in the finals.

McIngvale's 3½ somersault was a first for a woman, but she hopes it won't be a last. "I think," she says, "that we (women) tend to limit ourselves at times. Any athlete can put a mental limit on himself or herself, and before long that limit becomes a reality. There are a lot of things we haven't done yet that are possible."

Despite McIngvale's enthusiasm for reaching new horizons, she remains a realist about the abilities of women in head-to-head competition with men. Recently she was invited by CBS-TV to compete against men's champion Phil Boggs on the "Battle of the Sexes" telecast. She turned down the offer rather than endanger her amateur status, but quickly points out that, amateur status or not, she wouldn't have cared to participate. "I don't ever want to have to compete against Phil Boggs," she says adamantly. "There is no way I can beat him. He's much stronger than I am."

Today Cindy McIngvale gives little thought to ending her career. "I think it is a little foolish to put an exact limit on yourself. For years, athletes have labored under a preconceived notion that at a certain age you either burn out or your body quits functioning. You can talk to some so-called diving experts, and they'll tell you that after age twenty-four, you begin losing some of your strength. I'm twenty-six now and stronger than I've ever been, so it's hard for me to buy that line of thinking."

She does, however, feel it is necessary for an athlete occasionally to take time to do an honest self-evaluation.

"For instance," she says, "I don't feel that right now is the time for me to make any commitment for the 1980 Olympics. If in 1978 I'm still doing well and I'm enthusiastic, I'll make the decision." There was a time, she continues, "when I thought the Olympics were everything. They get in your blood, you know. And, of course, the primary objective was the gold medal. Now, though, I have to believe that the whole Olympic experience is, in the long run, more important than winning a gold medal. Sports has too much else to offer to make not winning a gold medal a sign of total failure.

"When diving is no longer fun," the two-time Olympian says with a wide smile, "I'll know it's time to quit and find something else to do." There is good reason to believe, however, that such a time is still a long way off. A backyard barbecue on Sundays will just have to suffice for rest and relaxation.

DANNY THOMPSON

Infielder, Texas Rangers

THE 25,000 FANS on hand at Arlington Stadium applauded mildly as Danny Thompson stepped to the plate. It was his first appearance in a Texas Rangers uniform after having been traded just a few days earlier from the Minnesota Twins, a team he had played with for the past six years. Now, at age 29, in the middle of the 1976 major league baseball season, the former Oklahoma farmboy was starting over again. It was a situation not new to him.

The fact that he had traded his Twins uniform for the Rangers colors was hardly the kind of news that makes headlines. In fact, he had come to Texas as part of a sweeping trade which had seen the Rangers, pennant contenders but in need of additional pitching help, get standout Minnesota pitcher Bert Blyleven. Thompson had been included in the deal almost as an afterthought. Because of injuries, illness, and problems with the Minnesota management, Thompson's career as an American League infielder had had its ups and downs. Of late there had been more downs than ups.

Thus it was that Rangers fans paid little attention when he was announced as the starting second baseman. It was common knowledge that regular Lenny Randle had been bothered by a variety of nagging injuries. Manager Frank Lucchesi, they assumed, would allow Randle a little rest and relaxation while Thompson filled in. After all, one of the Dallas newspapers had referred to him as "an obscure infielder thrown into the Blyleven trade at the last minute." No reason, then, to expect miracles.

Even when he singled off Detroit pitcher Bill Laxton in his first time at bat his accomplishment drew little more than polite applause.

But for Thompson it was an important moment. This was an important game, in fact. He felt his career had been dealt a revival by the trade and he was nervously impatient to prove himself. Maybe Texas fans were not turning cartwheels about his move from the Twins to the Rangers, but Thompson was. For the first time in longer than he cared to remember, confidence had sprung back into his life. His morale which had suffered over the past seasons had taken a new turn. All he had needed was a chance to prove himself. Texas offered that opportunity.

The Rangers management had convinced him that it felt he was a player whose talents could help them toward a desired league title, maybe a spot in the World Series. When Danny O'Brien, general manager of the Rangers, had called him in his Minnesota apartment to discuss the possibility of his move to the Rangers, he had come right to the point. He first told the infielder that Texas wanted him, then asked how much he was making with the Twins. Thompson was embarrassed to tell O'Brien his salary was only $27,500 after six years in the majors. O'Brien, aware that Thompson had engaged in several salary disputes with the Twins front office, then asked what the highest figure he had requested from Minnesota during contract negotiations had been. Thompson told him he had hoped to earn $36,000.

"Agree to play with us," O'Brien told him, "and we'll start you at $38,000. That's more like what you're worth." Danny Thompson did not need to give the matter further thought. The figure represented several things to him. Obviously, it meant more financial security but, equally as important to an athlete, it meant he was going to be paid a salary to which he felt his abilities entitled him.

On the night of 4 June 1976, the new career of Danny Leon Thompson began.

The sharp single to left in his first time at bat would be but a hint of what was in store. In the fourth he came up with two Rangers on base and cracked a three-run homer. As he slowly trotted the bases, Rangers fans began getting to their feet. The cheering grew louder and louder. By the time he crossed home plate a full-fledged standing ovation for the new Rangers infielder was underway.

Before the night was over Thompson had rapped out four hits, played flawless defense, and was clearly the star in the Rangers' 14–3 drubbing of the Tigers. Danny Thompson had found a home, a new starting place for his major league career—a career many felt would come to an abrupt, possibly tragic end when it was discovered on the last day of January in 1973 that he was suffering from chronic granulocytic leukemia.

It was to have been one of those routine prespring training checkups all ball players are required to take. Originally Thompson's visit with Twins' physican, Dr. Leonard Michienzi, had been scheduled for February first, but not wanting to celebrate his twenty-sixth birthday in a doctor's office, he had arranged to get it over with a day earlier.

Four days after Dr. Michienzi conducted his examination he placed a call to Thompson. "Danny," he said, "I know you've got things to do, but it is important that you meet me at the hospital tomorrow so we can run some additional tests."

Puzzled, then a bit frightened, Thompson agreed to be there. "Why?" he asked.

"Danny, have you been sick recently? Any infection?"

"Nothing," Thompson replied.

The next afternoon, the blood test taken, Thompson sat in the small reception room awaiting the results of the exam. Time crawled. And as it slowly passed, the young man who had assumed himself to be just another healthy athlete looking ahead to the upcoming baseball season, felt a gnawing in his stomach. Something was wrong. He had seen it in Dr. Michienzi's face the minute he had walked into the office.

The doctor finally appeared with the test results. Thompson's white cell count was up to 25,000. Normal is between 5,000 and 10,000.

"You're sure you haven't been sick lately?" the doctor again asked. Thompson again assured him that he had not even had a cold during the winter. He had never felt better in his life.

"Let's go to the cafeteria and have a cup of coffee," Dr. Michienzi suggested. "Then you'll have to come back up for another test. I want to take a bone marrow sample from your sternum."

"What will that tell you?" the concerned Thompson asked.

"Danny, we're checking for leukemia."

The word thudded against his brain. Leukemia. How? Why? Suddenly his mind boiled with questions. Was he going to die? What should he tell his wife Jo? Would he be able to play ball for another season? How much time did he have left?

Just as quickly his thoughts turned to the positive approach. He was an athlete, therefore in better condition than most men his age. He didn't smoke. He had taken care of himself physically all his life. No one as healthy as he was could have such a dreaded disease. It was, after all, just a test.

But a painful one. First, he was given a shot of Novocain to dull the pain, then a hole was drilled in his breastbone. Finally, a bone marrow specimen was extracted with a long needle. The blinding pain was like nothing Danny Thompson had ever experienced.

It was a Friday. The test results would not be complete until the following Monday. Thus began the longest weekend of his life.

Thompson waited until mid-morning the following Monday, then placed a call to the doctor's office. "Doc, this is Danny. Are the tests back?"

The doctor came straight to the point. "Danny," he said, "you've got leukemia. I think it would be a good idea if you and your wife came by the office this afternoon so we can talk. I'll explain it all to you then."

What he would explain was that Thompson had a "slow" type of the disease. There was no immediate danger that he would die or even have to give up baseball. He also suggested an immediate visit to the Mayo Clinic to visit Dr. Murray Silverstein, an expert in leukemia research.

"Thanks to the physical you took," Dr. Silverstein told him, "this is the earliest stage I've ever seen with this type of leukemia. Most people have had the disease for three, sometimes four years before they begin to feel tired or anemic and consult a doctor.

"How active the leukemia becomes is determined by your white cell count. Right now you're at 20,000. We won't even begin treatments until they reach the 100,000 range. My suggestion to you right now would be to just try and forget about the leukemia and begin concentrating on having a good season with the Twins."

Danny Thompson, then, was left with two options: He could sink into worry and self-pity about the blow recently dealt him; or he could live with the problem, put it aside as best he could, and go about his business of being a ball player. He chose the latter.

A devout Christian, Thompson returned to his apartment home with his wife and they talked about the problem. It was decided that his parents back in Oklahoma should know, but there was no use saying anything to their daughter Tracy at this point. She was still too young to understand. Danny and Jo Thompson talked quietly for hours: about the disease, about what the doctor had told them, about past hardships and how they had managed to overcome them.

"Since the time I accepted Jesus Christ," Thompson says, "I've tried to put my life in his hands. My first inclination was to pray to him and say, 'Lord, don't do this to me. Quick, make me well again so I can get to spring training.' But I knew that wasn't the thing to do, that he didn't work that way. Finally, I said to him, 'Here I am and here are my problems. Use me in any way you want to. I know that you've got a plan for me and will let me know what it is when the time comes.' "

It was impossible to put the thoughts of leukemia out of his mind, but Danny Thompson chose not to give up on his dream. He hoped he would one day be selected to the American League All-Stars. He would go back to work on that goal as soon as spring training opened.

During his boyhood days in Kansas, James Thompson had been an athlete of considerable ability. As a schoolboy in Elkhart, Kansas, he had run on the same track team with the famed Glenn Cunningham, a man who would go on to set a world record for the mile, and he had quarterbacked the football team. But he excelled at baseball; this was his obsession. An outstanding catcher, he received an offer to play professionally for a team in Wichita, Kansas, but not having a car and being unable to arrange for a ride to the team's training camp, he never got the dreamed-of chance at pro ball.

He made sure, however, that his son had the chance

he had been denied. By the time Danny Thompson
reached Little League age, the family was living in tiny
Capron, Oklahoma, where the elder Thompson owned
and operated a combination grocery-restaurant-hardware
store. On Saturdays his wife would drive young Danny
the twelve miles to the larger community of Alva where
he played Little League ball.

And while he had many of the same chores to which
most boys raised in a rural environment are exposed, the
young Thompson was seldom required to help out when
there was a baseball game to be played. At one time or
another, James Thompson had extolled the virtues of
athletics to every one of the eighty residents of Capron,
pointing out the fact that he felt it vitally important that
a boy be allowed to pursue sports to the fullest if he
showed an interest.

Danny Thompson showed an interest. It was his older
brother, Jimmie, who washed most of the dishes at the
family restaurant while his kid brother was off in some
vacant lot playing ball.

In retrospect it must be noted that it was time well
spent. At age fifteen, while playing American Legion
ball, he was scouted by the New York Yankees and
offered a contract upon graduation from high school.
The elder Thompson, however, was not that eager for
his son to become a professional ballplayer. First, there
was the matter of an education. His son turned down
the Yankees' offer and instead accepted a scholarship to
play baseball at Oklahoma State University in nearby
Stillwater.

By his senior year he was a collegiate All-American
and received a $20,000 bonus from Minnesota and a
minor league contract earning him $500 per month
while playing for St. Cloud, Minnesota, in the Northern

League. It was the first step toward a goal he had set for himself at age fifteen—to be a major league ballplayer.

In 63 games with St. Cloud in 1968 he hit a respectable .282, performed well defensively, and moved up to Class AA Charlotte of the Southern League where he was named the all-star shortstop. He continued to improve, hitting .302 and gaining the necessary confidence and poise demanded of a major league candidate. As the 1970 season began it was felt by the Minnesota management that he needed just a bit more seasoning so he opened the year as shortstop for the Class AAA Evansville farm club.

Then, at mid-season, the hoped-for call came from Minnesota. The time had finally arrived to move up to the Twins. The club's regular second baseman Rod Carew was sidelined with an injury. Though Danny Thompson had not played the position since Little League days, he was suddenly the first team second baseman for a major league team. He played the final 96 games of the year with the parent club and despite rookie mistakes and a .219 batting average, it was generally felt he was in the big leagues to stay.

"How many rookies," he chides, "do you know who make it into the Baseball Hall of Fame in their first year in the big leagues?" His reference was to a September event against Oakland when A's pitcher Vida Blue pitched a no-hitter against the Twins. The box score, which included Thompson's name, was immediately forwarded to Cooperstown.

Still Thompson was established as a member of the Minnesota Twins—perhaps not always a member in good standing, but a solid fixture with the club nonetheless.

Almost from the beginning, however, there were

problems. Thompson (shifted from second to shortstop and even third base on occasion), never felt comfortable, as if he had a permanent spot in the Twins infield. He made errors and was benched for long periods of time early in his major league career. Nagging injuries complicated his problems. His hitting fell off, suffering from stretches of inactivity brought on by manager Frank Quilici's refusal to put him in the starting lineup. A mushrooming personality conflict developed. And each tenure on the bench added damage to Thompson's ego. He was confident in his ability as a ballplayer but knew well that only by playing regularly would he overcome his problems with errors and hitting slumps.

In 1972 it appeared that he was well on his way to moving into a more comfortable position. Unhampered by injuries and encountering little pressure from Quilici, he played regularly and ended the year with a .276 batting average. Though he was not selected, there were those who felt he should have been named to the All-Star team.

Then, in 1973, came word of his leukemia. New questions arose in the minds of the Twins management. Club president Calvin Griffith and manager Quilici, upon hearing of Thompson's problem, assured him that for as long as he was able, he was a starter in the Twins infield. Yet when the team reported to spring training in Orlando, there were six new faces battling him for his job.

That is how it would be for the remainder of his stay in the Twin Cities. Despite the fact the leukemia offered no visible problem, Thompson was increasingly looked upon as a dispensable member of the club. Though he would receive the coveted Hutch Award in 1974, voted annually to that major league player who "best exemplifies the fighting spirit, desire and character of the late Fred Hutchinson" (a major league pitcher and manager from 1939 to 1964), his horizons as a professional seemed drastically reduced as each day passed.

In 1975 he committed twenty-six errors and was in and out the Twins lineup again. Rumors were afloat that he was up for trade, that the club was considering giving him his outright release, or that the club was desperately searching for a replacement at shortstop. The fans and the press, frustrated by the Twins' spotty showing, joined the anti-Thompson bandwagon. By the end of the trying season he was certain his career as a ballplayer was fast drawing to a premature end—at least so far as the Minnesota Twins were concerned.

No one, it seemed, had even taken notice of the fact that his .270 batting average for the year ranked him second among the American League shortstops. It was his defensive shortcomings which disturbed the Minnesota front office, the fans—and Danny Thompson.

"I got to the point," he admits, "that I was hoping they would hit the ball anywhere but toward me. After hearing for three years that I couldn't play shortstop, I guess it wore me down to a point where I began to believe it a little myself. My confidence seemed to have disappeared."

That is history now. The Danny Thompson playing in the infield for the Texas Rangers is a new man, one with confidence, poise, and a renewed enthusiasm for the game.

"I'm more relaxed now," he says. "I feel the people I'm working for now believe in me. They've given me a new chance, a new outlook.

"Sometimes God works in mysterious ways. Just when

you feel you've been put to the test about as long as you can hold on, he steps in and lends a hand. He's given me more second chances than anyone I know of."

Not only have Thompson's baseball fortunes taken a turn for the better. So has his daily battle with leukemia. Through a regular series of shots it appeared in 1975 that the disease had been arrested. His white blood cell count now remains at a controlled 16,000. For two years he had lived in quiet fear that the signs of deterioration might begin to show, that his baseball career would come to a premature end for the simple reason that his body would no longer perform the functions necessary for a professional athlete. That fear is no longer with him. Or if it is, it is even better concealed than it used to be.

He has become something of a champion to many suffering from leukemia. Regularly he receives letters from fans, young and old, offering encouragement or making him aware that the manner in which he has coped with and fought against the disease has been an inspiration to them.

There is every reason now to believe that he will be able to play ball for some time to come, to have plenty of seasons remaining in which to pursue his goal of making the All-Star team.

Many nights like his first in a Texas Rangers uniform and that goal might well just become a reality.

On December 10, 1976, less than two months after the completion of the season, Danny Thompson died in a Minneapolis hospital, a victim of the leukemia he had so courageously battled.

JANET LYNN

Five-Time U.S. Women's Figure Skating Champion

SHE LOOKS MORE like the girl next door or maybe a pixie-cute high school cheerleader than history's highest paid woman athlete. Yet blonde, hazel-eyed Janet Lynn, five feet and one-half inch of grace and charm, reached that magic plateau at the tender age of twenty after having already won five United States women's figure skating championships and earned a bronze medal at the 1972 Winter Olympics in Sapporo, Japan. Upon her return home she signed a three-year contract with the Ice Follies, a pact which would earn her a staggering $1.5 million. A camera firm, certain that her wholesome charm would benefit its sales, added another six figures to her new-found wealth, signing her to a one-year personal appearance contract. A Japanese soft drink firm agreed to pay her $100,000 to advertise its product.

In retrospect, one can only wonder what she might have been offered had she not missed out on the gold medal which virtually everyone felt she would win that memorable February night in Sapporo.

The 8,000 fans on hand in the colorful new Olympic Arena had been captivated by the young American even before she skated to the center of the ice to begin the demanding routine which she hoped would gain for her recognition as the top woman skater in the world. The beaming smile on her face gave no evidence of the pressure which weighed heavily on her slight shoulders.

Through the early stages of her program she was a picture of perfection, her blonde hair flying forward with each dip and turn, her arms outstretched, poetry in motion. Even the most critical of judges was hard pressed to detect a flaw in her performance.

Then it happened. Going into a flying sit spin, a relatively easy maneuver which she had successfully negotiated in numerous competitions, she fell to the ice. And while it would be the miscue that erased her chances of winning the gold medal, it would also be the split second in her athletic career which made her a favorite of sports fans the world over.

Courageously, she quickly climbed back to her feet and completed her routine, giving no visible evidence of disappointment, no sign that the fall had interrupted her concentration. Her routine finally completed, she skated to the sidelines as the fans rose to give her a standing ovation. The judges obviously had been equally impressed and awarded her high scores despite the fall, scores good enough to win her the third place medal.

"I guess," she says, looking back on the moment, "that the whole world groaned when I fell. People everywhere were watching on television and a lot of them, I suppose, simply could not believe that Janet Lynn, one of the favorites to win the gold medal, had fallen.

"Really, I didn't even have time to be shocked about it. All I knew was that the next maneuver on my schedule was a double axle and I jumped up as quickly as I could and went into it. Then came the slow part of the program and that's when it dawned on me what I had done. I just decided that the only thing to do was skate the rest of the program and enjoy myself and do as well as I possibly could."

The judges, who make their decisions on both technical merit and artistic impression, dealt the young Illinois native high marks. For technical merit she received seven 5.9s and two 5.8s while for artistic impression she earned six 5.9s, two 5.8s, and a perfect 6.0 from the Swedish judge.

"Of course everyone who competes does so in hopes of winning," Janet says, "but as I stood there on that awards stand I was nothing but happy as I accepted my huge, two-inch-wide bronze medal. I knew I had done my best and that was what the Lord had wanted me to do."

It was a moment which would mark a memorable end to an amateur career filled with hard work, awards, championships, and recognition as one of the most devoted Christian athletes in sports history.

"Competitive skating," Janet is fond of saying, "helped me to grow up. It's easy to let success go to your head, to begin thinking you're something you really aren't. And I'm human so I had to fight against those kinds of feelings. In doing so I had to try hard to live a Christian life instead of just talk about it."

She is more open and vocal about her religious beliefs than many athletes partly, she says, because the demands of travel, performances, and personal appearances leave her so little time for formal religious activities. "I try the best I know how to express my Christianity through my performances on the ice," she says.

Janet Lynn Nowicki (her last name was dropped when she began competing, a concession to the show business aspect of figure skating) was too young to know that her life would be given direction at the age of two and one-half when her father took her ice skating with the Cub Scout pack with which her mother worked. She admits that she personally has no true recollection of that winter day in 1955 when she tried, with little success, to keep her balance. "My parents tell me that I took to skating immediately, though," she says. "They said I would fall and refuse to let anyone else help me up. They say I laughed every time I fell and then bounced up and tried it again."

Before long she was teaching herself to skate backwards and perform leaps and spins learned from watching older, more experienced skaters.

"It was fun," she says, "but at first it was really no big thing. Neither I nor my parents had any reason to believe I was destined to grow into an Olympic skater. In fact, looking back, I can honestly say that skating has never been the sole driving force in my life. Of course, I've devoted a lot of hours to practice and have made the same sacrifices that any athlete must do to stay in good condition, but I never felt skating was important enough to let it crowd everything and everybody out of my life.

"Skating has always been a fun thing for me. I was given a talent to develop and I've worked hard to make the most of my gift. But I've worked equally hard to maintain the other interests that are a part of living life to the fullest. Church activities, friendships, parties, dates, movies—all the things that are a part of growing up—have been important to me."

From that first shaky afternoon on the ice, Janet's skating career moved at a rapid pace. At age three and one-half her mother enrolled her in an ice skating school. By the time she was in kindergarten she had advanced to private lessons. At age six she came under the tutelage of Miss Slavka Kohout who had been the junior ladies national runner-up in 1946 and was regarded as one of the world's outstanding skating instructors.

Aware that their daughter had a rare talent, the Nowickis would drive Janet from Chicago to the Wagon Wheel Ice Palace in Rockton, Illinois. The trips, made each Tuesday, Friday, and Saturday, covered 200 miles. The training schedule was rugged, tiring, and expensive, but Janet's parents today realize the effort and expense were well worth it. "I don't think we were ever pushy parents," Mrs. Nowicki says, "determined to make our child a champion athlete no matter what her feelings were about the matter. We simply realized that she had a talent, was interested in developing it, and did all we could to help her along."

By the time Janet was a second grader she was entering skating competitions. And with the entry into competition came even more sacrifices on the part of her parents. Her father sold his interest in a Chicago drug store at a loss and moved his family to Rockford to be closer to the Wagon Wheel Ice Palace in Rockton. He became manager of a Rockton drug store and, after settling into the community, he and his family joined the Lutheran church. Janet, though not yet quite eight years old, began to listen closely to the sermons. "For the first time," she says, "I began thinking—really thinking—about the Lord's Prayer which I said every night before I went to bed. I began trying to understand what it really was all about. That was one of the first steps in the growth of my faith."

As her faith grew so did her skating talent. Miss Kohout, a demanding yet gentle coach, wasted little time pushing her star pupil into competition against skaters considerably older. By the time she was nine years old Janet was skating against teenagers and making impressive showings.

It was 1966 when she accomplished her first major skating victory. Though only twelve and standing just four feet feet, six inches, she wowed the judges and fans at the Berkeley, California, National Junior Girls' Championships, winning the title over a field which included numerous girls four years her elder. "I was,"

Janet recalls, "still taking things like my white teddy bear with me on trips."

Two years later she became the youngest member of the U.S. Olympic team which would compete in the Winter Games in Grenoble, France. She had won a berth on the team, placing third to nineteen-year-old Peggy Fleming and twenty-year-old Tina Noyes. Despite being ill with the flu during the competition, Janet placed a respectable ninth against the best women skaters in the world. A week later the flu had developed into strep throat but the fourteen-year-old Miss Lynn still managed to place ninth in the World Figure Skating Championships.

There would be no medals, no headlines, for her first efforts against international competition, but the experience would prove to be invaluable.

The following year she skated to an upset victory in the U.S. National Skating Championships in Seattle and then won the North American Championships in Oakland, California. At the World Championships she moved up to fifth. Janet Lynn, now a fixture in the skating world, the youngster with a future which seemed to have no boundaries, was maturing as an athlete as well as a person. And she was developing a unique philosophy toward her competive endeavors: "I skate," she would repeatedly tell inquiring reporters, "because I love to and I want to try to radiate that love to other people."

It is something she managed to do with unparalleled success, right up through her bronze medal performance at Sapporo.

Regardless of one's dedication, however, long years of amateur competition take their toll on the spirit and desire of an athlete. The eagerness to endure long, demanding practices wanes and the competitive edge dulls. By the time the Ice Follies extended their lucrative offer, Janet Lynn was already seriously considering retirement from amateur athletics.

A year after turning professional she said, "I wish I could somehow go back and talk to all the ego-trippers in amateur skating and make them aware that winning isn't everything. Someday, they'll find out, it doesn't really matter all that much. Gold medals are nice but they aren't the most important things in life."

She is, then, unique. Not only in her grace and ability as a skater but in her remarkably mature attitude toward life as well.

In November of 1975 asthma forced her out of the Ice Follies spotlight, out of skating. Probably forever. Ironically, the type asthma from which she suffers is induced by exercise. Today she can take a little neighbor girl skating for her birthday or can go skiing with her family or even take ballet lessons which she enjoys. But the hard training necessary to perform professionally is something else.

"My manager tells me I should go back to the show and just skate short numbers," she says, "but I'm not going to just go out and skate for the money. Sometimes even now I go out to the rink and try to do some jumps and, of course, my timing is way off. I still get really mad at myself. I miss it, but there's no way I'm going to skate again professionally and not be able to do my best.

"You know, looking back, what I loved most about it all, the times I enjoyed most were those when I was practicing alone, without anyone there to push me hard, and I felt all sweaty and stretched out. Like I had gone the limit that day on my own."

Her breathing problems actually had begun before her appearance in the '72 Olympics. They became progressively worse during the early stages of her professional career. "My coach finally told me," she says, "that I would get to a certain point in my training and then not be able to go any further."

By the time she left the Follies she was taking nearly a dozen different asthma medications, including cortisone, seven times a day. "Finally," she says, "I just decided I couldn't do it anymore, knowing I was going to cough my guts out after every performance."

Yet despite the premature end of her career Janet Lynn is a contented person. She now has time to do things she had no time for while in constant training. Recently she reached yet another milestone in the maturing cycle, marrying long-time boy friend Rick Solomon. The ice skating pixie who just yesterday seemed to be every mother's little dream girl, the teenage darling of the sports world, is a grown woman now.

She often speaks at religious rallies and expresses delight that her biography, *Peace and Love,* has sold almost 100,000 copies and been translated into several foreign languages. It is just another avenue she has opened to share her faith in God with people throughout the world.

Today she seems reconciled to the fact that her professional skating days are over. For Janet Lynn there will be no more competitions, no more applause from thousands who come to rinks and arenas to watch her skate through her ballet-like programs.

"It was," she says, "a very special time in my life. One I will never forget."

Special is a proper adjective for Janet Lynn.

JIM RYUN

Miler

IT WAS ONE of those made-to-order days that seem
rarely to come to the world of sport. Seldom had
Mother Nature been so cooperative, as if eager to do
her part on an afternoon that was, by careful design,
destined to go down in sports history. The late summer

California temperature stood at a comfortable 75 degrees and there was but the slightest hint of wind. The conditions for an attempt on the world mile-run record were as ideal as one could hope for.

Young Jim Ryun, a freshman student at the University of Kansas, a youngster already being hailed worldwide as possibly the greatest miler in the sport's history, would attempt to bring the world record for his specialty back to the United States after a twenty-nine-year absence. Adding a touch of irony to the anticipation of this July day in 1966 was the fact that the last American to hold the mile-run record had been Glenn Cunningham who had accomplished the feat when he, too, had been a student at Kansas.

Now had come Ryun, the nineteen-year-old running prodigy, the rail-thin Topeka, Kansas, native who had bewildered the track world by running sub-four minute miles as a schoolboy, who had earned a spot on the 1964 United States Olympic team while still a high school junior, who had already competed against and defeated most of the world's great veteran distance runners.

As a teenager he had run past athletic milestones with the same relaxed ease he had displayed running past opponents. All that was left to be done before he could officially be acclaimed as the best miler in the world was to break the record. That, he had let it be known, was the reason for his being in Berkeley, California, on this particular Sunday.

Thus a track meet which just weeks earlier had faced the possibility of being cancelled had suddenly become one of the most eagerly awaited of the season. Originally it was to have matched the top U.S. competitors against a national team from Poland, but the Poles, upset over the American involvement in Vietnam, had issued an eleventh hour announcement that they were not coming. Meet sponsors, faced with possible financial disaster, met in emergency session and decided to go ahead with plans for the meet, matching the top American runners in each event. More important, since the meet would no longer boast international flavor, officials decided to switch from the planned metric distances popular in Europe to yards which are more familiar to U.S. track fans. Instead of the 1,500 meter run, the metric equivalent to the mile, the program would call for the mile run.

As soon as word of the switch reached Kansas, an excited Jim Ryun placed a long distance call to meet director Sam Bell. "Mr. Bell," the modest youngster said, "I'd like to take a shot at the world record."

With that short, to-the-point conversation the meet which had been floundering in the possibility of failure had suddenly taken on renewed importance. Of course, it would have the full complement of events which are standard to all major track and field meets. But, Sam Bell knew, this particular day would be remembered for a single event. Years after the meet had passed into the history books track and field enthusiasts would reflect on what happened that day.

It came to be known simply as The Berkeley Mile, one of the most incredible achievements in the carefully chronicled history of sport.

The crowd of 15,000 was buzzing with excitement as the entrants in the mile run were introduced. There was applause for Cary Weisiger, the sub-four-minute miler from the San Diego Track Club; for Richard Romo, the young University of Texas graduate who would become the first from his native state ever to break the four-minute barrier; Oklahoma State's Tom Von Ruden; Oregon's Wade Bell; and Pat Traynor, the veteran distance runner from the 49ers Track Club. Then announcer Dwain Esper called attention to the lanky young man who was pulling off his sweat suit. An echoing ovation greeted Jim Ryun as he approached the starting line, seconds away from his bid for athletic immortality.

Each of the competitors would play a part in the drama. All were aware of Ryun's goal and knew that a fast pace throughout the race would be of utmost importance. They had agreed to help, to set a record pace through the first three quarters of the race and then let the young Kansan go the final lap on his own.

A sudden hush fell over the crowd as the starter called the runners to their marks. Then at the crack of the gun Von Ruden jumped into the lead with Ryun close on his heels. The runners, all finely conditioned, sprinted effortlessly down the straightaway of the clay and decomposed granite track. The cheering had begun anew, not to subside until the race was completed.

It had been decided that if a record was to be possible Ryun would have to complete the first quarter mile in 58 seconds. Von Ruden, running as if a clock was plugged into his brain, paced his friend and rival through the first 440 in 57.99. As the announcer made the fans aware of the record pace, causing a new burst of cheering, Romo jumped into the lead to set the pace for the second lap. Ryun, still running effortlessly, matched him stride for stride.

He passed the half mile mark in 1:55.5, still on schedule. Romo, his mission accomplished, relinquished the pace to Bell as the runners charged into the third lap.

Going into the backstretch Ryun began to move,

pushing himself to an even greater pace, past Bell and into the lead. Now, he knew, it was up to him. In a field of six of the top American milers, Jim Ryun was now alone. For the last lap and one-half it would be a battle against bone-crushing fatigue and the stopwatch. The crowd cheered even louder as he opened up a seven-yard lead over the field.

In the stands they sensed a record in the making. None of the 15,000 had ever seen a world record set in the mile, the glamor event of American track. Fully aware that they were witnesses to history in the making, they yelled encouragement to the lanky youngster gliding down the backstretch, the noise almost drowning out the announcement of the time for three quarters. Those who did hear the time—2:55.3—burst into screams. All that was needed now was a 58-second last lap and the record would be broken. Famed for his last lap sprints, Ryun had never run his last quarter slower than 58 seconds in a major race.

As he entered the last lap, the competition now falling far behind, Ryun found himself thinking that perhaps a 3:50 mile was possible. Pain was now setting in, his powerful legs began to ache, his arms grew heavy and his lungs burned. Yet, almost incredibly, he increased his pace as the crowd rose to its collective feet to cheer him through the final tortuous lap. He pressed the pace around the curve, faster than usual because now every fraction of a second counted. This was no time to miss the record by a fraction of a second. He had come too far to fail now.

With 300 yards to go he tried again to pick up the pace, to go into the long homestretch sprint for which he had become famous. Digging deep into his physical and mental reserves, he found that the lift was not there.

The blistering early pace had taken its toll. There would be no blinding sprint for the tape this day, just a struggle to maintain his current pace and not bow to the extreme fatigue which was engulfing his body. As he raced out of the last curve and into the final straightaway there was little outward evidence of the pain. Four years of daily training in the early mornings of Kansas winters and the heat of sweltering summers had prepared him physically for this moment. Yet there is no training program to make one ready for the kind of pain the youngster was experiencing as he powered his way through the final yards of the race.

In the stands people were jumping up and down, slapping each other on the back in premature celebration. Meet officials lined the track, waving their white caps, yelling encouragement.

Ryun, oblivious to all the commotion, drove his arms hard, in long reaching swings, pumping his weary legs until he was past the finish line. It was over. As wild celebration broke out he walked slowly around the curve, his head pounding, his legs aching. He was walking slowly down the backstretch when the official announcement came over the loud speaker. The official time was 3:51.3. The world record was back in America. A group of track experts calculated that Ryun had run the distance eighteen yards faster than anyone had ever done before.

Meet officials asked him to take a victory lap, something he had never done before. Embarrassed yet thrilled with his accomplishment, he jogged a lap barefoot as he received a standing ovation.

Within twenty-four hours he would be front page news throughout the world. In Paris, a newspaper used two full pages to report the record race. UPI sportswriter Joe Sargis wrote that "young Jim Ryun stood all alone today as perhaps the greatest track and field hero of all time."

Before the tumult and shouting would die down he would be given an award by the Amateur Athletic Union for the most outstanding single performance in the world for 1966. The Helm Athletic Foundation would name him the outstanding amateur athlete in North America, and he would win the Sullivan Award as America's top amateur athlete by the largest voting margin in the award's thirty-eight-year history. Heady attention, indeed, for one so young.

"Goals," Ryun says today, "are worthwhile and the work necessary to achieve them is good for a person. I still have to wonder, though, about the effect of reaching a goal like breaking the world's record. All the attention, the press making you sound like some kind of superman, people asking for your autograph. It's very easy to let your values get thrown out of whack."

It was a problem he worried about even as a schoolboy back at East High in Wichita. When it became increasingly obvious that he was going to become the first high school athlete ever to break four minutes in the mile he went to his minister and asked him if he felt it proper to pursue such a lofty goal.

The answer was one that was to stay with Ryun throughout his career: "Jim," the minister told him, "if you don't set your goals high, you'll never reach them. If one is going to go into this sort of thing, if you are going to try to be the best miler in the world, you, as a Christian, must dedicate yourself to doing the very best you can. Just don't ever get to the point where you feel you can achieve greatness by yourself. Remember that you have to have God's help."

"I was seventeen when he told me that," Ryun says. "I understood what he was saying then, but as I grew older it made even more sense. Running has been a big part of my life. It has brought me a great deal of satisfaction. I've been able to travel all over the world to compete, and I've achieved some things, reached some goals. Still, it is not a lasting thing. Records get broken. Someone faster will always come along and get the attention of the press. I will always consider running an important and satisfying part of my life. But not as important as the more lasting things—my Christian faith and my family."

In the years that followed the Berkeley Mile, Jim Ryun's athletic career would develop into one of peaks and valleys. In June of 1967 he would lower his own world record to 3:51.1. Yet the following year, competing in the devastating one and one-half mile high altitude of Mexico, he would fall short in his bid to win a gold medal in the Olympic 1,500 meters, finishing second to Kenya's Kipchoge Keino. He would shock the track world in 1969 by stepping off the track, failing even to finish his race in the National AAU championships in Miami. "My priorities are changing too fast for me to keep up with them," the weary Ryun told reporters. "Suddenly I no longer feel capable of or interested in running."

Discouraged by the long list of minor yet nagging injuries which had been plaguing him, miffed by the sudden sharp criticism from the press, and facing new responsibilities as a husband, he announced his retirement at a time when many felt he should be at the peak of his career. It was impossible to believe that Jim Ryun, the teenage folk hero of track and field, the young man who had brought his sport into the national spotlight, would never run again.

His retirement lasted nineteen months.

In retrospect, the complex young man had, by his own admission, created unbearable pressures for himself. "People," he would say, "have made me into a super-something and I felt I had to constantly push myself to be that imaginary person."

It would not be the constant urging of friends or his longtime coach Bob Timmons or even his own personal desire to reach newer heights as an athlete which would eventually bring him back to training. That credit goes to his wife, Anne, a pretty former Kansas State coed Ryun had met while competing in a track meet on the KSU campus. "When he decided to give up he was very unhappy," Anne recalls, "but after a while he saw that not running was making him even more unhappy. What he had to do was make up his mind that he would forget the outside pressures and run and compete for his own satisfaction and not worry about the demands of others."

"I had always felt that I had a God-given talent and a responsibility to develop it," Ryun says. "So I thought about it and prayed about it. I asked God to show me the best way to return to athletics. I also asked that he give me the strength to face the pressures which had built up in my mind."

Thus in January of 1971 he returned to training, working with the same dedication and enthusiasm he had maintained as a teenager. But he continued to falter in competition. For every good race he ran there would be two bad ones in which he would run poorly or not even finish. In an attempt to work himself back into top condition he moved to Eugene, Oregon, the home base of many of the top distance runners in the nation. The relocation just created a new problem. The high pollen count wreaked havoc with Ryun's hay fever, causing him to lose a great amount of workout time. Next stop, Santa Barbara, California. Still things weren't falling into place. He continued to struggle, seldom showing any competitive sign of the Jim Ryun of old. Early in 1972, a new Olympic year, he placed last in the Meet of Champions in Los Angeles, running the distance in 4:19, a time he had not run since his sophomore year in high school.

The Ryuns moved back to Kansas. "I kept thinking that it might be my last chance to try for an Olympic gold medal, so I decided to go back to my old coach and my old surroundings and see if that would help," Ryun says.

It did. Slowly he began rounding into shape. The hay fever problems disappeared and confidence began to return. Eventually he qualified for his third trip to the Olympic Games, winning his specialty in the Olympic Trials. At last things were looking up. Jim Ryun, in top form and running well, appeared ready to accomplish the one goal he had failed to achieve in two previous Olympiads.

Then in Munich, Germany, came the ultimate anguish. In a qualifying heat of the 1,500 meter run, Ryun tried to pass two runners late in the third lap of the race. With about 550 meters to go, a tiring Mohammed Younis of Pakistan accidentally moved into the American runner, striking him in the torso with his arm.

Ryun stumbled backward into Billy Fordjour of Ghana. As they fell, Fordjour's knee struck Ryun's throat and jaw, causing him to lose his breath. In his fall, Ryun also injured his hip, strained his right knee and left ankle. He lay on his back for several agonizing seconds then courageously climbed to his feet and completed the race. Far back among the finishers, however, his time was not good enough to advance him to the finals.

Standing on the infield, his knee bleeding, his vision blurred by pain and tears, Jim Ryun was faced with the grating realization that his last hope for an Olympic gold medal was gone. Once again disappointed and disillusioned, he began again to ponder the end of his athletic career.

"When I left for Munich," he recalls, "we had $200 in the bank and I had no real idea what I was going to do for a living when I got home. You have no idea how guilty I felt on the way back from Munich. Anne, who had been teaching school to support us while I trained, was pregnant, and all I could think about was the need for me to forget competing and find a way to make us financially secure."

Already regarded as an outstanding photographer, he hoped to pursue photography as a career.

But then came a meeting with a man named Michael O'Hara, a former Olympic volleyball participant and a Southern California businessman who was forming an organization he planned to call the International Track Association. The country, he was convinced, was ready for professional track. But what it needed to succeed was a headliner, a name star who could capture the attention of the fan being introduced to a new professional sport. Suddenly, the roller coaster life of Jim Ryun was taking another upward swing. What O'Hara and the ITA were offering him was the best of two worlds. He could continue his competitive career and also insure a handsome income for his family.

He signed a contract which called for a bonus as well as a regular salary for his promotional services on behalf of the ITA. Then, of course, there would be the prize money for running in the forty meets on the pro circuit.

There are those who will insist that the formation and success of professional track caused a transformation in Jim Ryun. Never noted for being relaxed, much less glib around members of the media, he suddenly became an outgoing young man who delighted in referring to himself as a "professional jock." At age 26, the 6'-3", 160-pound sports world phenom finally became comfortable with himself.

"For years," he says, "I devoted my entire life, all of my energies, to running, training, and competing. I missed a lot of things, a lot of the simple daily pleasures of life. I've finally come to the realization that it's no sin to relax and enjoy things. A lot of the pressure is gone."

But there would eventually come the time to quit competing for good. The world of distance running has no George Blandas or Gordie Howes. Ryun, the young Kansan who held the world record at his specialty for eight years, knew this. But he no longer worried about the time it would come to an end. In March of 1976, Jim Ryun called a press conference to inform the members of the sporting media that it was time for him to retire. The announcement was made with a smile, a cheerfulness which needed no apologies.

"God blessed me with an ability to do some things others were unable to do. Why he picked me to be a successful runner, I'll never know. But I'm thankful he did. Maybe I've had my ups and downs, but it's been a wonderful life."

Listening to him talk, one gets the impression that no matter what the future holds, the bad times are past for the young man whom history will look back upon as the one who put the sport of track and field into the nation's athletic spotlight. It's a designation not even an Olympic gold medal winner can claim.

HARRY CORDELLOS

Marathon Runner

THE IDEA HAD BEGUN to take shape in the fall of
1968 as Harry Cordellos, a soft-spoken information
clerk for San Francisco's Bay Area Rapid Transit, sat
listening to his brother tell of the thrill he had experienced while competing in the annual Bay-to-Breakers

road race. "He made it sound so invigorating," Cordellos recalls. "And quite obviously he had felt a great sense of accomplishment from having completed the seven and three-quarters mile race. It had given him a tremendous lift. My brother made running sound like such a joy that I knew immediately I wanted to have a try at it."

There were, however, few members of Cordellos' family or circle of friends who stepped forward to lend encouragement. Sure, it was commendable that he would entertain the idea of launching into a training program which would enable him to join in with a nation which seemed to be going crazy about running, that he would want to put himself through the physical agony necessary to properly condition himself for long distance racing, but the idea offered a unique problem for Harry Cordellos.

Since birth he had been blind.

"I had never been allowed to compete in any kind of athletics," he recalls. "First, because I am blind and then because of a heart condition I had as a youngster. There were quite a few people who tried to talk me out of it—and their intentions were good, for my benefit— but I just decided that it was time for me to break out and have a go at something I really wanted to try."

Switch now to the 1975 Boston Marathon, a grueling twenty-six-mile race which ranks today as something of a distance runner's Super Bowl.

It occurs each year on the anniversary of Paul Revere's historic ride, luring a montage of entrants ranging from the Walter Mittys of the world to gifted runners with Olympic credentials. Mixed into the annual mob scene is a healthy number of doctors, lawyers, bricklayers, guys next door, an occasional housewife, kids with nothing better to do, and several dogs named Spot.

It's 26 miles, 385 yards of agony and ecstasy which begins at high noon on the village green of suburban Hopkinton, Massachusetts, and is finished in downtown Boston's Prudential Center. For his efforts, the winner receives a floral wreath, a traditional bowl of hot beef stew, and the quiet satisfaction which comes from having triumphed in the oldest foot race in American sports history. For the thousands of losers there will be bunions, blisters, possible heat prostration, pain, and finishers' medals for all those who, regardless of elapsed time, manage to complete the taxing course.

Among those lined up for the 1975 running was Harry Cordellos. In two hours, fifty-seven minutes and forty-two seconds he would cross the finish line with an achievement many had felt impossible. His performance still stands today as the fastest marathon ever accomplished by an American runner competing under the handicap of total blindness.

He had gone to the starting line alongside friend and running partner, Commander John Butterfield, U.S. Navy, who had come from his home in Rhode Island to help Cordellos in his attempt at establishing the Boston record. For the first mile of the race, until the shoulder-to-shoulder crowd began to clear and the running became less hazardous, they ran with their hands clasped, Butterfield leading the way.

Once the field began to stretch out and the danger of being jostled and knocked to the ground was past, they ran side-by-side, maintaining constant elbow contact.

Born blind, the forty-year-old Cordellos underwent a series of operations as a youngster and for a brief period during his early teens had partial vision. It lasted only long enough, he remembers, to see many of his friends active at their various sports activities. His vision disappeared again, however, in the late 1950s. Thus today he runs in total darkness.

"Running," he says, "is the greatest thing in the world. There isn't a day that goes by that I don't thank the Lord for giving me the opportunity to do what I'm doing now. I'm not saying that I didn't have a good life before I began running, but certainly it has added another dimension."

Needless to say, there is no longer any effort to discourage Harry's competitive efforts. Rather, he is met with encouragement everywhere he turns.

"I run daily," he says, "but how many miles I'm able to do depends on who else might be in the park running at the time I get there. Some weeks I get in forty or fifty miles, others no more than fifteen or twenty. It all depends on who's around and what kind of schedule they have planned. If I run into someone planning to do speed work on that particular day, that's what I do. I might go out to practice, feeling I need to have a long run but someone handy might want to do hill running. That's okay with me; I do hill work too. There are a lot of really nice people in San Francisco who are always willing to let me run with them and offer me constant encouragement.

"Oh, at first there were a few who felt it might be a little dangerous but once they saw me around and realized I was serious—and capable—they changed their tune. I've fallen a time or two, usually when running on a dirt or gravel road where the footing isn't an easy thing even for someone who can see, but it's never been a real problem, except for the amount of time I lost.

"Every time I line up for a race I just pray to God for a safe run and the courage to finish," he says.

Courage, it would seem, is not something in which

Cordellos has been found lacking. He competes in forty to forty-five races a year. One of his most recent accomplishments of note was a fifth place finish in the Honolulu 50-Mile Run on Memorial Day in 1977.

"He is," says sometimes partner Butterfield, "an incredible person. It's been a pleasure to run with him. An inspiration, really. I ran with him recently at the White Rock Marathon in Dallas and never had so much fun. He told me before the race that he had been having trouble with a sore muscle in his foot and hadn't been able to properly prepare for the race, but they had invited him to run and he didn't want to back out.

"For the first fifteen miles we ran along with him singing and acknowledging the cheers of the crowd. But the miles finally began to take their toll on him and he developed a pretty bad stitch in his side with about six miles to go. But he never broke stride. He ran with a lot of guts. It wasn't the first time I've seen him do it."

The first thing Cordellos did after completing the White Rock affair was to seek out marathon director Dr. Kenneth Cooper and apologize for not having posted a better time. He had completed the course in three hours, thirteen minutes and fourteen seconds—which was better than about half the 1,200 competitors managed to do.

For one who was forbidden to participate in any kind of school activities because of his handicap, Cordellos has of late become quite a busy sportsman. In addition to his running, he has been waterskiing since 1958, has a best nine-hole golf score of 55, has bowled a 129 game, and has recently become involved in cross-country snow skiing.

But it is marathoning which has become his enduring passion. "I love running, competing, and meeting peo-

ple who share the same feelings I have about the sport,"
he says.

The sport, and the people who participate in it, has
also developed a strong feeling about Harry Cordellos.
In every sense of the word, he is one of its champions,
an overcomer.

Carlton Stowers

writes a regular column for *The Dallas Morning News* and is assigned to cover the Dallas Cowboys football team. He has written for such publications as *Sports Illustrated, TV Guide, Sport, Golf Digest, Boys Life, People Weekly,* and others.